# Cultural Sociology

*Series Editors*: Jeffrey C. Alexander, Ron Eyerman, David Inglis, and Philip Smith

Cultural sociology is widely acknowledged as one of the most vibrant areas of inquiry in the social sciences across the world today. The Palgrave Macmillan Series in Cultural Sociology is dedicated to the proposition that deep meanings make a profound difference in social life. Culture is not simply the glue that holds society together, a crutch for the weak, or a mystifying ideology that conceals power. Nor is it just practical knowledge, dry schemas, or knowhow. The series demonstrates how shared and circulating patterns of meaning actively and inescapably penetrate the social. Through codes and myths, narratives and icons, rituals and representations, these culture structures drive human action, inspire social movements, direct and build institutions, and so come to shape history. The series takes its lead from the cultural turn in the humanities, but insists on rigorous social science methods and aims at empirical explanations. Contributions engage in thick interpretations but also account for behavioral outcomes. They develop cultural theory but also deploy middle-range tools to challenge reductionist understandings of how the world actually works. In so doing, the books in this series embody the spirit of cultural sociology as an intellectual enterprise.

**Jeffrey C. Alexander** is the Lillian Chavenson Saden Professor of Sociology and Co-Director of the Center for Cultural Sociology at Yale University. From 1995–2010, he edited (with Steven Seidman) the *Cambridge Series on Cultural Social Studies* and from 2004–2009 (with Julia Adams, Ron Eyerman, and Philip Gorsky) *Sociological Theory*. Among his recent books are *The Civil Sphere* and *The Performance of Politics: Obama's Victory and the Democratic Struggle for Power*.

**Ron Eyerman** is Professor of Sociology and Co-Director of the Center for Cultural Sociology at Yale University. His areas of research include social theory, trauma, and memory, and he has taught undergraduate and graduate courses on these topics. He is the author of *The Assassination of Theo van Gogh: From Social Drama to Cultural Trauma*.

**David Inglis** is Professor of Sociology at the University of Aberdeen. He is founding editor of the journal *Cultural Sociology*, published by Sage. His recent books include *The Globalization of Food* and *Cosmopolitanism*.

**Philip Smith** is Professor and Co-Director of the Yale Center for Cultural Sociology. His recent books include *Why War?*, *Punishment and Culture*, and *Incivility: The Rude Stranger in Everyday Life* (coauthored) among others.

*Interpreting Clifford Geertz*
Edited by Jeffrey C. Alexander, Philip Smith, and Matthew Norton

*The Cultural Sociology of Political Assassination*
Ron Eyerman

*Constructing Irish National Identity*
Anne Kane

*Iconic Power*
Edited by Jeffrey C. Alexander, Dominik Bartmański, and Bernhard Giesen

*Seeking Authenticity in Place, Culture, and the Self*
Nicholas Osbaldiston

# GLOBAL INJUSTICE SYMBOLS AND SOCIAL MOVEMENTS

THOMAS OLESEN

Thomas Olesen (2011). "Transnational Injustice Symbols and Communities: The Case of al-Qaeda and the Guantanamo Bay Detention Camp," *Current Sociology* 59(6): 717–734.

Thomas Olesen (2012). "Global Injustice Memories: The case of Rwanda," *International Political Sociology* 6(4): 373–389.

Thomas Olesen (2014). "Dramatic Diffusion and Meaning Adaptation: The Case of Neda Agha Soltan," in Donatella della Porta and Alice Mattoni (eds.), *Spreading Protest: Social Movements in a Time of Crisis*, pp. 71–90. Colchester: ECPR Press.

First published in 2015 by
PALGRAVE MACMILLAN®
in the United States—a division of St. Martin's Press LLC,
175 Fifth Avenue, New York, NY 10010.

Where this book is distributed in the UK, Europe and the rest of the world, this is by Palgrave Macmillan, a division of Macmillan Publishers Limited, registered in England, company number 785998, of Houndmills, Basingstoke, Hampshire RG21 6XS.

Palgrave Macmillan is the global academic imprint of the above companies and has companies and representatives throughout the world.

Palgrave® and Macmillan® are registered trademarks in the United States, the United Kingdom, Europe and other countries.

ISBN: 978–1–137–48116–0

Library of Congress Cataloging-in-Publication Data

Olesen, Thomas, 1969–
    Global injustice symbols and social movements / by Thomas Olesen.
        pages cm
    Includes bibliographical references and index.
    ISBN 978–1–137–48116–0 (hardcover : alk. paper)
        1. Social movements. 2. Social justice. 3. Symbolism—
    Political aspects. 4. Signs and symbols—Political aspects. I. Title.

HM881.O45 2015
303.48′4—dc23                                          2014036603

A catalogue record of the book is available from the British Library.

Design by Newgen Knowledge Works (P) Ltd., Chennai, India.

First edition: April 2015

10 9 8 7 6 5 4 3 2 1

*For my girls—Lene, Alma, and Nora*

# CONTENTS

# SERIES EDITOR'S PREFACE

WE ARE ALL AWARE OF POWERFUL IMAGES OF INJUSTICE THAT COME to us from outside of ourselves, circulating round the globe—a young Iranian women, Neda Agha Soltan, lies murdered on the ground, open-eyed, with blood streaming from her head; an incarcerated African hero, Nelson Mandela, towers over the heads of his jailers, seeing the future of his people's triumph; the Rwanda genocide becomes the Holocaust of contemporary time; Guantanamo Bay a torture chamber of injustice.

All these are deeply moving, but until Thomas Olesen's work, they have gone unexplained. Olesen calls them "global injustice symbols," and he researches four cases of how they emerge and become cultural powers on a global social scale. He also provides a sociological theory that explains how this new form of global power comes about.

In these empirical and conceptual efforts, Olesen brings together late Durkheim, the strong program of contemporary cultural sociology, and a distinctive take on social movements. The contemporary relevance of Durkheim's religion theory has been limited by its focus on simple societies. Olesen discovers how powerfully condensed symbols can emerge from the more fragmented social terrains of contemporary societies, providing meaning and motivation for social groups and communities of conviction, and on a global scale.

How exactly such global symbols emerge is Olesen's special concern. He looks at communicative infrastructure and cross-national cultural schemas but his principal focus is activist groups. They are the agents that make global symbols possible. They believe in the symbols themselves, and they want the world to share their faith, not only for moral but also for strategic reasons. From tacit knowledge, activists know that only by projecting powerfully shared symbols can global movements for social change succeed.

Methodologically, Olesen provides a rich demonstration of how symbols can be studied in concrete and dynamic ways. Empirically, he shows that, at least in the communicative domain, powerful elements of a civil sphere are indeed emerging on a global scale. Events unfold on local levels in real historical time, but they can be transformed into symbols whose myths unfold on a global scale. The innocence of victims is essential, and their charisma grows out of their cultural power to make amends.

A deeply innovative work of the sociological imagination, Global Injustice Symbols significantly deepens our understanding of our times.

JEFFREY C. ALEXANDER

# Acknowledgments

As any other project this one started several years ago as a loose idea and more or less free-floating concept. As it began to materialize as something more than this I struggled to find a unifying core that would unite my growing inventory of cases and analyses. In this difficult phase of the project I benefited enormously from the comments and support from others. My stay at Gothenburg University in May 2012 at the Forum for Civil Society and Social Movement Research (CSM) was a central and defining moment. Invaluable insight and, not least, motivation was provided in an unusually constructive and hospitable atmosphere by Carl Cassegård, Christoph Haug, Abby Peterson, Geoffrey Pleyers, Håkan Thörn, Stellan Vinthagen, Matthias Wahlström, and Åsa Wettergren. Papers were presented at numerous conferences and meetings along the way, but two deserve special mention. The positive and critically constructive reception at the conference on Processes of Radicalization and De-Radicalization at the Center for Interdisciplinary Research, Bielefeld University, April 6–8, 2011, convinced me that the core idea was not perfect but worth pursuing. The ECPR Joint Sessions workshop on the Transnational Dimension of Protest, March 11–16, 2013, organized by Donatella della Porta and Alice Mattoni, gave me invaluable ideas and motivation for guiding the project into its final phase. I sincerely thank all the participants at these events for engaging so thoughtfully with the project. You know who you are. Numerous others have given direction and motivation to the project along the way. They are Jeffrey Alexander, Lorenzo Bosi, Donatella della Porta, Alice Mattoni, Enuga S. Reddy, Dieter Rucht, and Philip Smith, as well as a number of anonymous reviewers for *American Journal of Cultural Sociology*,

*Current Sociology, International Political Sociology,* and *Research in Social Movements, Conflicts, and Change.* Finally I wish to thank my colleagues at the Department of Political Science and Government, Aarhus University, and especially the Sociology section, for providing such a friendly and professionally stimulating academic "home." Special thanks are owed to Lone Winther for thoroughly reading and setting up the final manuscript. I also wish to thank the Danish Council for Independent Research for a grant that made several of the case studies possible.

Writing about and turning the pain and misery of others into a study object is a strange business. It is impossible not to be drawn emotionally into these stories that often demonstrate the dark side of humanity (and equally impossible, at times, to avoid feeling like an academic parasite objectifying and turning suffering into a product and career pathway). But while there is certainly enough in the book to make you despair and doubt, it is also testament to a powerful moral-political core at the heart of our (global) society. It may not be big enough, not powerful enough, but it is there. And it is there for us to maintain, expand, and write about. I dedicate this book to my wife Lene and my daughters Alma and Nora for reminding me of that every day—and in so many different ways.

AARHUS, DENMARK
September 3, 2014

# CHAPTER 1

# GLOBAL INJUSTICE SYMBOLS

ABU GHRAIB, CHARLIE HEBDO GUANTANAMO BAY, MY LAI, Malala Yousafzai, Mohamed Bouazizi, the Muhammad cartoons, Neda Agha Soltan, Nelson Mandela, Rodney King, the Rwandan genocide, Sharpeville—at first glance the names on this list do not seem to have much in common. Yet, despite the glaring differences in character, time, and place, they share one thing: they are all *injustice symbols*. *Injustice* symbols because they refer to events and situations that involve perceived moral and political transgressions and have motivated debates about collective perceptions of right and wrong; and injustice *symbols* because they have, instantly or over time, attained universalized meanings that transcend their spatiotemporal root. The book rests on two guiding arguments. First, all of these symbols have been created in and through *social movements*. In perhaps slightly awkward terms, social movements are both consumers and producers of injustice symbols. They not only draw on and invoke existing symbols but also contribute to the formation of new ones. Second, they are all, to varying degrees, of course, *global* injustice symbols shaped by political dynamics beyond their local/national origin and containing meanings for audiences outside of this context. Our collective moral and political maps are dotted with such symbols. We create them as recipients and carriers of shared moral and political meanings and visions and use them to make sense of and contextualize the present. Late modern and global societies thus continue to understand themselves and communicate through symbols in ways that do not fundamentally differ from premodern and modern societies (Alexander, 2010; Alexander, Bartmanski, and Giesen, 2012; Alexander and Mast, 2006; Alexander and Smith, 2003). What nevertheless distinguish contemporary symbols are precisely the two elements specified above: their often political and global nature. The book is about such *global injustice symbols* and revolves around three questions: *How are global injustice symbols formed? How are they employed by political actors and for what purposes? And to what extent are they reflective of a global society?*

With these arguments and questions, the book addresses a lacuna in the literature on global social movements and global civil society, which has seen a small avalanche of works arrive since the late 1990s (e.g., Anheier, Glasius, and Kaldor, 2001; Anheier and Themudo, 2002; Bob, 2005; Crack, 2008; della Porta, Kriesi, and Rucht, 1999; della Porta and Tarrow, 2005; della Porta et al., 2006; Guidry, Kennedy, and Zald, 2000; Juris, 2008; Kaldor, 2003; Keck and Sikkink, 1998; McDonald, 2006; Olesen, 2005; Pleyers, 2010; Reitan, 2007; Smith, 2008; Smith, Chatfield, and Pagnucco, 1997; Smith and Johnston, 2002; Tarrow, 2005; Teune, 2010).[1] In none of these works do we find any systematic engagement with social movements' capacity to employ and produce injustice symbols at a global level.[2] Rather, the predominant focus has been on institutions (political opportunity structures), resources, networks, communication (strategic framing), and organization. While studies within these traditions have significantly advanced our understanding of global social movements, they leave two research avenues and theoretical traditions unexplored. First, it might be argued that the strand of social movement theory least adapted to a global level of analysis is the cultural, dramatic, and emotional turn of the last 10–20 years within social movement studies (e.g., Alexander, 2006; Eyerman, 2006; Flam and King, 2005; Goodwin, Jasper, and Polletta, 2001; Jasper, 1997, 2009; Johnston, 2009; Johnston and Klandermans, 1995). Second, the existing literature as a whole suffers from a macro-sociological deficit, which keeps us from addressing the wider question of the relationship between global social movements and society (but see Thörn, 2006, and Wennerhag, 2008, for some important deviations). The book seeks to integrate these two concerns in the concept and study of global injustice symbols. Such a focus particularly enables us to bring out three aspects: (1) *global injustice symbols concern the infusion and ascription of collective values and meanings*; (2) *as a result, global injustice symbols are intimately related to (global) society and the social*; (3) and *the symbolic process is movement driven and consists of a mix of dramatic, emotional, and strategic elements*. These emphases do not imply a turn away from the political. As is evident from the term "injustice," and as will be clear in the coming chapters, global injustice symbols are *all about politics*. What the book insists on is to analyze how the political is rooted in and shaped by deep-lying cultural and political themes and schemas and how these dynamics increasingly occur at a global level.

With its emphasis on socially anchored themes and schemas, the book draws significant inspiration from the strong program in cultural sociology (e.g., Alexander, 2004a, 2006; Alexander and Smith, 2003). While cultural sociology has developed an impressive amount of research, its predominant emphasis has been *national* society. Cultural sociology seeks to establish analytical accounts identifying the productive and reproductive interaction between actors and the value systems of society. Such an exercise is considerably easier at the national than at the global level. At the former level, research can draw on and tap into century-long histories ripe with defining moments, core symbols, and identifiable political cultures, which, moreover, are well documented by historical and sociological research. To the extent that there are common histories, values, and belief systems at the global level, these are evidently "thinner," more intangible (but certainly not absent or irrelevant as argued by Smith, 1995), and, as a result, harder to theorize and analyze. This is not to suggest that theorization and analysis of globality is absent in the field (e.g., Alexander, 2007, 2012) but rather that it lacks a systematic empirical and theoretical agenda. By providing a clear empirical reference point and an engagement between theory, concepts, and data over several case studies, the study of global injustice symbols and social movements in the present book hopes to be able to advance such an agenda within cultural sociology.

The book is structured around four chapters and case studies that refract the concept of global injustice symbols in different ways. Chapter 2 talks about global *political iconography* with an empirical point of departure in Nelson Mandela's political career. Chapter 3 analyses the role of injustice symbols in the constitution of global *grievance communities* within political Islam, the empirical pivot being the Guantanamo Bay detention center. Chapter 4 discusses the 1994 Rwandan genocide as a global *moral memory* that continues to guide and inform the politics of the present. And chapter 5 addresses the process of global *dramatic diffusion*, that is, the globalization of local violent events, with a focus on Neda Agha Soltan, a young Iranian woman killed during protests in Iran in 2009. While the case chapters are considered to make independent analytical, theoretical, and conceptual contributions, there are obvious connecting lines between them. For example, grievance communities are typically defined by political icons and undergirded by shared moral memories. Similarly, dramatically diffused events may turn victims into political icons and anchor them in collective memories. As the following theoretical and conceptual discussions will hopefully show, these are just a few examples of how the themes, concepts, and chapters of the book may be theoretically and analytically interrelated and combined. The case chapters are followed by a concluding chapter, which employs the case studies to open up a broader political-sociological discussion of the extent to which global injustice symbols reflect a global society and public sphere. This discussion will also take a critical position highlighting issues of power, inequality, conflict, bias, and adaptation. The remainder of the present chapter lays out the general theoretical and conceptual groundwork for these upcoming analyses and debates. It begins by outlining the intimate relationship between injustice symbols and (global) society. This is followed by a detailed theoretical, conceptual, and definitional discussion of each of the core concept's constitutive parts as well as of the concept of global social movements. Finally, it presents some notes on methodology and approach.

## INJUSTICE SYMBOLS AND SOCIETY

This section is divided into four subsections. The first subsection out-lines the Durkheimian inspiration informing the concept of global injustice symbols (the concepts of symbol and injustice symbol are defined in detail in the next section). The second expands and develops this line of thinking with concepts drawn from framing and cultural theories within social movement studies. The third seeks to couple these insights to the discussion of global society. The final subsection concludes with an empirical illustration and a condensing figure.

### THE ROLE OF SYMBOLS IN SOCIETY

Some time ago, Charles Tilly (1978) famously dismissed a "useless Durkheim" as a theoretical source of inspiration for social movement scholars. He was right to do so in many ways. Durkheim's work, espe-cially the parts pertaining to anomie and social breakdown and dis-order, was an indirect or direct presence in the collective behavior tradition, which during the 1970s and 1980s came under increasing criticism for casting social movements in a predominantly irrational and apolitical light (see McAdam, 1982, for another pace-setting cri-tique). The new generation of movement scholars coming through in the 1970s and 1980s, many of them deeply inspired by the hectic movement activity of the 1960s and 1970s, wished to portray activists as genuinely political actors with strategies and agendas. The swift repudiation of Durkheim from the social movement circle during the 1970s and 1980s had much to do with his purported association with functionalist theory and, as noted above, with a view of social move-ments as symptoms of social irrationality and imbalance (Emirbayer, 1996). It can, of course, be debated whether such a strong reading of Durkheim was/is justified. This is another story, however. Rather, this book wishes to emphasize the continued relevance of what might be thought of as the cultural vein in Durkheimian sociology (e.g., Alexander, 2006; Smith and Alexander, 2005) for social movement studies—a vein that primarily springs from Durkheim's late work in *The Elementary Forms of Religious Life* (1912/2001). Of particular interest here, Durkheim in that work emphasizes the inextricable relationship between *symbols* and *society* (this connection has also been documented in anthropology, e.g., Geertz, 1973; Turner, 1967). For Durkheim, society thus rests on a set of shared values and meanings enacted in rituals and often inscribed on and expressed through symbols (the kind of symbols studied by Durkheim were mainly emblems, totems, and tattoos in non-modern societies): "Without symbols...social feelings could have only an unstable existence...But if the movements by which these feelings have been expressed eventually become inscribed on things that are durable, then they too become durable" (2001: 176). Slightly translated, it tells us that symbols are *carriers of collective values and meanings*. Symbols thus connect individuals and groups with society and the social. Recognizing and employing a symbol is to express adherence to a certain set of social values and meanings. This also has a temporal dimension in the sense that symbols serve to "transport" values and meanings across time and generations. Put differently, the study of symbols is the study of society, a window into how collectives understand themselves and their relation to the wider social world. Symbols are constructed via moral and political *binaries* (e.g., Alexander, 2011), that is, a positioning of actors and acts in sacred (not necessarily in a narrow religious sense) and profane categories that negatively define each other. The symbol thus represents what is seen as right and good by a collective and, directly or indirectly, what is considered wrong and evil. This dynamic, as will be developed below, is especially evident in *injustice* symbolization. As the concept clearly indicates this subset of symbols are forged through a moral-political identification of acts and actors that are *un*just (see also Smith, 2000).

Of course, Durkheim's thoughts on symbols were primarily developed based on his empirical observations of aboriginal societies in Australia. Yet, he clearly considered his insights to be generalizable to the level of modern and secular society. Accordingly, several strands of Durkheim's late work on religion have been adapted to the sociological analysis of modern societies (e.g., Alexander, 2004a; Alexander and Smith, 2003; Bellah, 1973) and social movements (especially, Alexander, 2006, but see also Emirbayer, 1996). The merit of this work largely lies in its ability to address the macro-sociological deficit identified earlier and, thus, in sensitizing us to a sociological point too often lost in the literature not only on global social movements but also on social movements in general: social movements simultaneously *draw on* and are important actors in the *construction* of the moral and political ideas and values that undergird society. Yet, despite the relevance of Durkheimian thought, the coupling between it and the study of social movements calls for some qualification and expansion. First, while symbols in Durkheim's work generally play socially *integrating* roles, symbols today are infinitely more complex. This is particularly the case with injustice symbols. Injustice symbols may and should still be thought of as *carriers of collective values and meanings*, but in the late modern (and increasingly global) world these are generally contested, politicized, and conflictive (elaborated below). Studying injustice symbols, then, opens up to the way collective values and meanings are politically negotiated and in constant flux. Second, Durkheim mainly focused on already existing symbols and their meanings and less on the processes of their *formation*. But symbols do not fall out of the sky. Nowhere does this aspect come out more clearly than in the relationship between social movements and injustice symbols. As argued above, social movements not only use and employ symbols but they also play key roles in their formation.

### POLITICAL-CULTURAL SCHEMAS AND MORAL SHOCK

The preceding arguments do not intend to claim that the social movement literature is devoid of reflections relevant for the study of injustice symbols. Two currents in particular offer a number of useful concepts and theorizations for advancing such an agenda and giving the rather general Durkheimian insights some firm theoretical and conceptual shape. The first current, the framing school, was established in the 1980s (Snow et al., 1986; Snow and Benford, 1988) as an antidote, or rather supplement, to the dominance of structural and rationalist theory in social movement studies, the goal being to highlight the communicative and interpretive activities of social movements. As a whole, however, the emphasis in much of framing research is on the question of strategy, efficacy, and the maximization of public resonance (see Goodwin and Jasper, 1999, for a critique). It is important to underline at this point that the approach taken in this book is not incompatible with a strategic approach; as will emerge below and in the chapters that follow, the activities surrounding injustice symbol formation and employment are often permeated by strategic thinking. The concern is rather that a focus on strategy risks blotting out the socially productive side of social movements. Despite these limitations, framing scholars do offer several useful ideas that essentially serve to draw out the connection between movements and society, for example, master frames (Snow and Benford, 1992), cultural resonance (Gamson, 1995), themes and counter-themes (Gamson and Modigliani, 1989), interpretive packages (Gamson and Modigliani, 1989), and metapackages (Gamson and Lasch, 1983). Sociologically speaking, all these concepts share a basic point that movement communication is always a *public-sphere*-anchored and *audience*-dependent dialogue with society (Alexander, 2006: 231) in which socially anchored values and meanings are invoked to give direction to and generate resonance for present claims. Injustice symbols are well suited to illustrate this dynamic because they entail a complex integration of the *particular* and the *universal*. The process of universalization, that is, turning a specific event or situation into something that represents and resonates with an existing moral and political horizon of meaning, can only occur through the communicative interaction with values and meanings already available in the cultural and political structure of society.

Building upon the framing tradition, the concept of *political-cultural schema* is introduced to capture this dynamic. By coupling the political and cultural two things are intended. First, the term "cultural" points to the essentially late Durkheimian idea that these schemas are anchored at a deep social level and that society is constituted in and by the way human actors invoke, create, and recreate such schemas. Second, the term "political" seeks to clarify that the kinds of schemas of primary interest in the context of social movements and injustice symbols are those that involve overtly political values and meanings. The relationship between injustice symbols and schemas is dialectical and reflects the distinction recurrently made between injustice symbol *formation* and *employment*. On the one hand, schemas contain injustice symbols that may be appropriated by movements in new spatial and temporal contexts (the employment side). On the other hand, schemas are the social "stuff" that injustice symbols are made from—the material used to universalize the particular (the formation side). This latter process is not a one-way street. When schemas are invoked for political purposes, they also potentially change (such change can involve extension, strengthening, and challenge) (for a related argument, see d'Anjou and Van Male, 1998; Hart, 1996; Williams, 2004). Schemas are not free floating and outside of human agency; they have sponsors (Gamson and Lasch, 1983; Gamson and Modigliani, 1989) and thus reflect certain *interests, power constellations,* and *self-understandings* (see, especially, chapters 5 and 6). Consequently, they are part of a wider public and discursive field in which they often stand in politically *competitive* relationships with each other (see, especially, chapter 3; see also figure 1.1).

As already noted in the introduction, the second current considered to resonate with the book's ambitions is the cultural turn in social movement studies in recent decades (especially, Alexander, 2006; Eyerman, 2006; Jasper, 1997, 2009). The major achievement of this turn has been its insistence on the *moral-political* dimension of social movement action. Injustice symbols are based on events and situations that entail some element of human suffering and unjust behavior toward others. As such, they are generally motivated by indignation or what Jasper and Poulsen (Jasper, 1997: 159–162; Jasper and Poulsen, 1995) call *moral shocks*. Moral shocks are events, situations, or conditions that challenge collectively and individually held conceptions of right and wrong, just and unjust (as such, the concept is closely related to that of trauma, which also points to events, situations, or conditions with profound impact on collective moral-political values; see, e.g., Alexander, 2004b, 2012; Eyerman, 2004; Eyerman, Alexander, and Breese, 2011). Moral shocks often have a *solidarity* dimension. In the late modern and global world, moral shock is typically a media dependent and constructed relationship between audiences and distant others in which suffering and injustice in one part of the world undergoes a scale shift (Tarrow, 2005) to become a concern for individuals and collectives in other spatial settings (Boltanski, 1999; Chouliaraki, 2006; Olesen, 2005, 2014; Silverstone, 2007). Moral shocks (and trauma) are never automatic. Rather, they are *created* and *amplified* through social movement action publicly highlighting and exposing the injustice of an event or situation (Jasper, 1997: 161). This observation underlines how the moral dimension in social movement action is neither incompatible with, nor is it the opposite of, strategic and political action. The two often combine (Alexander, 2006; Jasper, 1997). Actors in social movements are quite conscious about the political-strategic potential in certain events and situations and utilize their dramatic and emotional elements to maximize visibility and resonance and to back up claims for political intervention and ameliorative action (see also the discussion on global social movements below).

It is important to emphasize that the term "moral-political" as it is used in this book does not necessarily mean "good" action elevated from the world of ordinary politics and based on some universal standard. Moral-political action is rather defined as action that reflects deeply held values about just and unjust. When a suicide terrorist blows himself up, it is a profoundly moral-political (and thus good) act for him and his organizational and political-cultural milieu, although for most audiences it will be qualified as unequivocally "bad" and evil.

INJUSTICE SYMBOLS IN GLOBAL SOCIETY

Up until this point, the discussion of injustice symbols and society has been rather general in nature and without a direct focus on their *global* dimension. The specific elements of global injustice symbols will be developed in the next section, but what is important at this stage of the argument is to outline the relationship between injustice symbols and *global society*. Looking back to the Durkheimian inspiration, Durkheim, for obvious reasons, had little to say about global society. The book concurs, however, with Alexander (2007,

2012) when he argues for the continued relevance of Durkheim's ideas even in today's increasingly global context. Thus, according to Alexander (2007: 372), globalization is not "something radically new" but rather "another step in the millennia long compression of time/space/meaning." Most globalization scholars have been concerned with the compression of time and space as expressed in increasingly rapid and border-crossing trade, travel, and communication patterns (Held et al., 1999). Others have opted for a sociological approach emphasizing how globalization is characterized also by a growing global consciousness (e.g., Robertson, 1992). In the quote above, Alexander refers to this latter aspect as, among other things, a compression of *meaning*: "There exist not only new technologies of movement and communication but more condensed and transcendent cultural logics, such as democracy and human rights that spread common understandings and structures of feeling more widely than before." The guiding macro-sociological argument of the book is that global injustice symbols are an empirical prism for studying this process of value and meaning formation at a global level (see also Waters, 1995). In Alexander's terms, they allow us to identify and analyze a *global civil sphere*. For Alexander the civil sphere refers to a society's *value core* (Alexander, 2006). By tentatively extending the concept to the global level, he suggests that such a value core may also be identified at the level of global society ("compression of meaning," "common understandings," and "structures of feeling") (Alexander, 2007, 2012). However, Alexander cautiously only identifies a *nascent* global civil sphere, which also lacks a strong regulatory and institutional framework (at the national level the civil sphere is institutionalized through a judicial and political system in which rights and solidaristic ideas are legally protected and firmly embedded). This book wishes to be slightly bolder and argues that the presence of global injustice symbols and global social movements are indicative of a well-developed and vibrant global civil sphere (even if it is not anchored in a legal and political framework comparable with those at the national level). It is of utmost importance to underline that the identification of a global civil sphere should not lead us to overemphasize harmony, homogeneity, and extension. To the contrary, and as discussed earlier, injustice symbols are highly political and thus often illuminate conflict, contestation, and power relations. This is perhaps even more pertinent at the global level. Thus, studying global injustice symbols is to study the *politics* (and, therefore, historical nature) of global society and the global civil sphere (the concluding chapter 6 critically elaborates on the concept of the global civil sphere and discusses it in relation to the *potentials* and *limitations* of global society).

In practical and concrete terms, global symbolic processes occur in a *global public sphere*. The global public sphere consists of four interconnected elements: (1) an "infrastructure" for communication made up by the media (television, newspapers) and interpersonal and intergroup communication technologies such as Facebook, Twitter, and other Internet-based platforms; (2) actors (including, not least, global social movements) utilizing this infrastructure to communicate and act across national boundaries; (3) cross-nationally and cross-regionally shared and available political-cultural schemas; and (4) globally dispersed audiences attentive to issues, events, and situations occurring in other national contexts than their own.

## ILLUSTRATION AND CONDENSATION

Let us conclude with an empirical and figurative illustration. Figure 1.1 condenses the basic theoretical concepts introduced above and their relations.

Considering the case of Malala Yousafzai, at the age of 15, on October 9, 2012, she was shot in the head by a Taliban gunman. At the time, Malala lived in the Taliban dominated Swat Valley in Pakistan. The assassination attempt had been preceded by her outspoken criticism of the Taliban's ban on girls' school attendance. The attempt generated immediate acts of protest in Pakistan and, soon, also reactions from activists, media, and politicians around the world. Malala was later flown to England to receive medical treatment; she is now a globally recognized figure in the struggle for girls' right to education. A fund to support this struggle has been established in her name and on July 12, 2013, she was elected to speak at a major

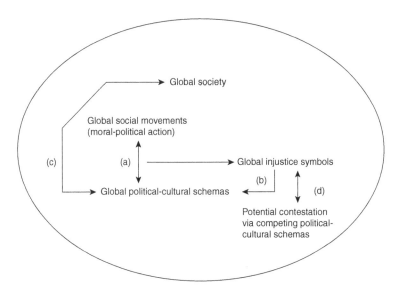

Figure 1.1    Injustice symbols in the global public sphere.

United Nations (UN) conference on youth and education. In the theoretical vocabulary outlined above, Malala is a *global injustice symbol* and was recognized with the Nobel peace prize in 2014. The singular event of her assassination attempt has come to represent (universalization) a wider global problematic of girls' lack of access to education due to political (as is the case in Taliban-dominated areas such as the Swat valley) or socioeconomic restrictions. The symbolization process occurred in an interaction between a global social movement (see below for an elaboration) and a global-society-anchored *political-cultural schema* stipulating gender equality as a basic and universal right and value (arrows "a" and "c"). The activities leading to Malala's symbolic status had a strong *moral-political* dimension that combined *outrage* and *moral shock* with a call for political action to address the problem. Underlining the dialectical nature of these dynamics, the Malala symbol is now a social-movement-produced element in the political-cultural schema on gender equality (arrow "b") and, in a wider sense, of global society (arrow "c"). The Malala symbol, however, has not escaped contestation. It has thus been interpreted from a different and competing political-cultural schema that portrays her symbolic status as a Western creation intended to delegitimize Muslim culture and challenge Pakistani national independence and identity (arrow "d").

## CONCEPTUAL AND THEORETICAL OUTLINE

This section offers a conceptual and theoretical unpacking of the book's core concept: global injustice symbols. This is followed by an exposition of how the concept of global social movements is understood and employed in the book.

### SYMBOLS

Defining symbols is a highly complex task. The concept straddles a number of scientific disciplines and is used in academia as well as in everyday parlance. The following tries to keep it in a short leash and focuses only on two overall themes considered especially relevant for analysis in this book: (a) universalization and displacement and (b) a typology of the empirical phenomena that underlie symbols.

*Universalization and Displacement*
Elder and Cobb offer a useful definitional starting point: a symbol, they say, is "any object used by human beings to index meanings that are not inherent in, nor discernible from, the object itself" (1983: 28). A symbol, then, consists of two basic elements: something empirical, an *object*; and the values, ideas, and meanings imputed to it by human actors (see also Bartmanski and Alexander, 2012). "Such symbols," Elder and Cobb continue, "serve to summarize and to condense experiences, feelings, and beliefs" (1983: 29), their meanings transcending the underlying empirical object. A symbol, in other words, combines and integrates the *particular* and the *universal*: the particular being the empirical object and the universal the wider meanings and values imputed to this object. Employing the vocabulary of the preceding section, the process of universalization is always grounded in existing political-cultural schemas. The focus on universalization, however, does not imply erasure of the particular (the object). A symbol is always anchored in and cannot interpretively depart too far from its

underlying object and empirical reality. It is a marriage of facts and meaning, as it were (as discussed later, contestations over injustice symbols often occur precisely around the empirical facts related to the object). Universalization implies that symbols have an inherent capacity for *displacement* and what Alexander (2004b) calls *analogical bridging* (see chapter 4). Two kinds of displacement are particularly relevant for the present discussion. *Temporal displacement* refers to the employment of a symbol in a new historical context. What is important here is not the temporal distance but rather that the symbol is invoked in relation to events other than those that originally produced it. As shown by Alexander (2004b), for example, the Holocaust injustice symbol was repeatedly invoked during the Balkan Wars in the 1990s. *Spatial displacement* refers to the employment of a symbol in a new geographic context. The term "apartheid" is thus frequently used in relation to other instances of perceived injustice, including, for example, Israel's presence in Gaza and the West Bank. As both examples demonstrate, temporal and spatial displacement often co-occurs.

Universalization and displacement suggests that we may think of symbols as *outcomes* (Olesen, 2013a). They are social "things" created by human actors that have acquired independent existence in the social world and therefore can be employed as a material and resource in a wide variety of temporal and geographic contexts. Yet, even if it makes sense to think of symbols as outcomes, they are never so in a fixed manner: first, as suggested, symbols may be challenged through the appearance of new facts about the underlying object; second, whenever a symbol is employed by human actors, it potentially acquires new meanings (this is particularly the case with temporal and geographic displacement). Symbols are inherently unstable and in a constant process of becoming.

### A Typology of Objects

As noted above, symbols always have an empirical object as their basis. There are three main objects with relevance for injustice symbols: events/situations, people/individuals, and images/photographs.

*Events and situations* refer to occurrences and conditions involving perceived instances of suffering and injustice. This is a broad category with at least four subcategories: violent person-events, massacres, genocides, and systematic repression. *Violent person-events,* as the term implies, refers to violence against "ordinary" individuals (all the other subcategories have a more collective character) considered innocent and undeserving of such violence. Within this category we find the cases of Malala Yousafzai, discussed above, and Neda Agha Soltan, shot and killed during protests in Iran in 2009 (see chapter 5). *Massacres* are defined as occurrences where a relatively large group of people related to each other through shared social, cultural, and political identities and characteristics are killed for political reasons by identifiable perpetrators over a short period of time and in a single locality. Examples of massacres that fit this definition would include the My Lai massacre in Vietnam, 1968, the Sabra and Shatila massacres in Lebanon, 1982, and the massacre at Tiananmen Square in China, 1989. *Genocides* also involve politically motivated killing of people with shared identities, but, in contrast to massacres, these have a much larger scale in terms of both geography and the number of people killed, are more systematic, and occur over longer periods. Examples here are the Holocaust and the 1994 Rwandan genocide (see chapter 4). *Systematic repression* does not necessarily involve the killing or wounding of groups or individuals (although it often does); rather, it refers to situations where a group of people with shared identities is systematically repressed and controlled by a state actor or other collective agent in ways that significantly limit their social, cultural, or political freedom. Examples within this category are South African apartheid (see chapter 2) and Israeli occupation of Palestinian territories. Imprisonment may also be considered part of this subcategory: for example, the Guantanamo Bay detention center (see chapter 3) and Robben Island where Nelson Mandela was incarcerated from 1964 to 1982.

Some *people/individuals* attain iconic or symbolic status through being associated with certain political and moral values and accomplishments. Of primary interest within the context of this book are individuals/icons related to social, cultural, and political struggles over democracy and human rights. Key examples are Nelson Mandela (see chapter 2), Aung San Suu Kyi, Dalai Lama, and, in a wider historical perspective, Mohandas Gandhi and Martin Luther King. Individuals within this category typically have a recognized leadership status for a collective and in relation to a specific political struggle. As such they are different from the above-mentioned category of violent person-events that mainly involve ordinary individuals with no or limited previous public status.

*Images* or *photographs* of suffering and injustice often acquire more or less independent status as injustice symbols (Alexander, Bartmanski, and Giesen, 2012). Nick Ut's 1972 photograph of a group of naked children fleeing from a napalm bomb attack at the village of Trang Bang achieved symbolic status in its own context of antiwar protests and remains well known almost 40 years later (Hariman and Lucaites, 2007). On September 30, 2000, a France 2 freelance cameraman filmed a Palestinian father and son (Mohamed al-Durrah) caught in crossfire between Israeli and Palestinian forces. At the end of the footage, the boy is seen lying over his father's legs, apparently dead from gunshots. The footage was circulated globally, giving rise to widespread condemnation of Israel's politics toward Palestine (Liebes and First, 2003) (the role of photography is expanded upon in the "Innocence" subsection below).

This typology of objects is an ideal typical one. In reality, the categories are often connected and part of what might be called *symbolic families*. For example, apartheid is a situation-based injustice symbol in its own right, but one widely understood through iconic figures such as, most notably, Nelson Mandela, but also Stephen Biko and Desmond Tutu. It is furthermore surrounded by a range of supportive event/situation-based symbols such as the Robben Island prison, the 1960 Sharpeville massacre, and the Soweto uprising in 1976. Some of these events/situations in turn are strongly related to certain photographs. For example, the Soweto uprising is intimately tied to the photograph (taken by Sam Nzima) of Hector Pieterson, a 13-year-old schoolboy, being carried in the arms of a student, with his sister running beside them, after being fatally shot by police during protests. These considerations also indicate that the event/situation category should be thought of as a *master category*. When, for example, an individual, ordinary as well as iconic (see above), attains symbolic status it is almost without exception connected to an event or situation (Aung San Suu Kyi to Burmese dictatorship, Neda Agha Soltan to a repressive Iranian regime, etc.). And when images and photographs gain independent symbolic status, they typically do so because they temporally "freeze" an unjust event and situation.

## INJUSTICE

Like the term "symbol," "injustice" is a multifaceted term. For the analyses in this book, three themes are of particular relevance: (a) the question of authorship and responsibility; (b) the often-contested nature of injustice; and (c) the determinants of injustice perceptions.

### Authorship and Authority

Injustice, at least in a political sense, refers to a relationship between human actors or between human actors and manmade structures, practices, and institutions that do not necessarily have clearly identifiable authors. Such relationships involve elements of authority (Moore, 1978). Injustice symbols thus typically spring from events or situations where authority has been exercised (and sometimes *not* exercised; see chapter 4) in ways considered unjust by a collective and where a relatively clear victim-perpetrator relationship has emerged. As discussed above, the element of authority is central to injustice symbol formation because it enables the establishment of universalizing causal links. Authority, at least as it is understood here, is thus always exercised on behalf of some wider social and political power arrangement. It is only when an object can be meaningfully related to and understood within such a context that it acquires universalizing potential.

The term "authority" is flexible and needs to be specified. We may usefully distinguish between *individual* and *collective* expressions of authority. Some injustice symbols are formed around events where identifiable individuals have committed unjust acts. Such acts, however, only become a potential foundation for injustice symbols if they can be contextualized within a *system of authority* (Snow and Soule, 2010). This also helps us distinguish between what we might call *private* and *public* injustice. An assault on an innocent pedestrian by a gang is obviously unjust, but unless it can be related to a system of authority it remains private and without strong symbolic potential. Such a link can be made if the assault, for example, can be plausibly represented as racially motivated and as such related to racism as a system of authority. When an Indian woman, Jyoti Singh, was gang raped in a New Delhi bus in December 2012 (she was left in a coma and later died from the assault), she rapidly achieved the status of an injustice symbol. While, in a simple sense, the assault was a common crime, it was immediately interpreted as an expression of a wider system of authority that devalues the role of women in Indian society. In June 2010, an Egyptian man, Khaled Said, was beaten to death by two policemen in Alexandria. His death became a key injustice symbol in the protests that toppled the Mubarak regime in early 2011. While the two policemen had acted independently, Said's death was widely seen as a symptom of impunity and brutality under Mubarak (Olesen, 2013b). In other cases, the events and situations underlying injustice symbols do not have individual authors in the same direct sense as in the cases above. *Collective* authors are typically states and institutions. The Guantanamo Bay injustice symbol (see chapter 3), for example, may be linked with individuals such as US president George W. Bush and other key political figures at the time of its inception, but for those imputing Guantanamo Bay with injustice meanings it is generally seen as the creation of the US government. Similarly, Nelson Mandela's imprisonment from 1962 to 1990 involved individual political decisions, but, ultimately, the author of his imprisonment was considered to be the apartheid state in a broader sense (see chapter 2).

As shown above, injustice symbols result from unjust *acts*. Often these acts are coupled with unjust *in*action. Our moral and political universe is based on expectations about how injustice should be avoided and, if it does occur, how it should be addressed. Such expectations are almost unequivocally directed toward local, national, or international political authorities. In the aftermath of the Rwandan genocide in 1994 (see chapter 4), debates thus raged not only over the apparent injustice of the genocide but also over the lack of international intervention to stop it. The Rwandan injustice symbol/memory was made up of both dimensions. Similarly, following the rape of Jyoti Singh in India, anger, as mentioned above, turned not only toward a sociocultural system of sexism but also toward the Indian political elite, which was accused of systematically neglecting a problem permeating Indian society for centuries.

## Contestation and Mutuality

Injustice is obviously not an objectively observable category. Consequently, when the term "injustice symbol" is employed it should be borne in mind that it is always injustice seen from the perspective of a *specific collective*. As such, injustice (and thus injustice symbols) is inherently contestable. Contestation may concern the empirical foundation of the injustice symbol. As noted elsewhere, all injustice symbols have an empirical base: that is, they are founded on observable events or situations entailing some kind of injustice. Such a dispute arose over one of the most famous visual injustice symbols from the Balkan Wars in the 1990s. In this footage we see a group of Muslim prisoners standing behind a barbed wire fence at the Trnopolje camp in the Prijedor region. However, critics later contested its status, arguing that what was portrayed as a concentration camp was in fact a refugee camp and that the "prisoners" were standing *outside* the barbed wire compound (for detailed accounts of the controversy, see Campbell, 2002; and Taylor, 1998: 60–63).[3] While the controversy over the Trnopolje camp footage occurred after the fact, the symbol formation process itself is often characterized by energetic attempts of *de-symbolization* (see chapter 5). De-symbolization is usually undertaken by authorities held responsible for an unjust event or situation. When the death of Khaled Said, mentioned earlier, began acquiring symbolic status in prerevolutionary Egypt, authorities issued various statements, some of which portrayed Said's death as a result of injuries he sustained when he collapsed after having swallowed a bag of marihuana. Egyptian authorities thus pursued a two-pronged de-symbolization strategy in which doubts were raised over the causes of Said's death and his moral character put in question (he was described as a drug user and military deserter) (Olesen, 2013b). De-symbolization is fraught with political danger, for authorities and may unleash *backfire* mechanisms (Hess and Martin, 2006). In the case of Said, his injustice symbol status was in fact increased by de-symbolization attempts as evidence was brought to the public that refuted authority allegations.

Backfire may also occur when authorities attempt to de-symbolize by making concessions in one form or another. No photographs exist of Mohamed Bouazizi's self-immolation on December 17, 2010; an event widely credited with triggering the Tunisian Revolution. Bouazizi did not die immediately from his wounds, but was hospitalized in the city of Ben Arous in a coma until January 4. As it became increasingly clear to Tunisian elites at the end of December that protests were gradually spreading to the national level, President Ben Ali visited Bouazizi in hospital in an attempt to dampen growing discontent. The photograph taken at this event shows Ben Ali standing over a comatose and mummified Bouazizi. What was probably seen as a photo opportunity for the president had an almost reverse effect. Immediately following a clash with police and municipal officers on December 17, Bouazizi, a street vendor, had approached city officials to have his confiscated wares and equipment returned, but to no avail. Now, after having set himself on fire and initiated a wave of protest, Bouazizi was finally granted an audience with power. Yet the terms of that audience were evidently laden with injustice. First, few in the viewing audience were likely to be convinced about Ben Ali's sincerity in a "meeting" that had been arranged only when elites felt the situation was slipping out of control. Second, the photograph depicted an awkward meeting between power and powerlessness: Ben Ali in a suit with his hands solemnly crossed and Bouazizi invisible in his bandages and unable to participate and formulate his frustrations. Even if Ben Ali was only responsible for Bouazizi's fate in an indirect manner, he nevertheless represented the social and political system that had produced Bouazizi's self-immolation. While present in the same physical space, the symbolic distance between Ben Ali and Bouazizi could hardly have been greater. The photograph and the terms of the meeting between Ben Ali and Bouazizi seemed only to increase the latter's innocence and moral stature, while at the same time, in a reverse proportional relationship, decreasing that of Ben Ali and the regime he represented (Olesen, 2013c).[4]

There is often a thin line between injustice and *justice* symbols. Paraphrasing a famous saying, one man's injustice symbol may be another man's justice symbol. The contested nature of injustice symbols thus points to their essentially *audience dependent* nature. The degree of contestability varies significantly between injustice symbols. Some injustice symbols are almost unanimously accepted. For example, few would dispute the empirical foundation and moral implications of the Rwandan genocide injustice symbol (see chapter 4). The Muhammad cartoons published by a Danish newspaper in 2005 is another story. The cartoons depicting the prophet Muhammad (such depiction is prohibited in some versions of Islam) became a rallying cry for aggrieved Muslims all over the world and has since been established as a core injustice symbol for, for example, Islamic terrorist organizations such as al-Qaeda (Olesen, 2014). What is interesting about the Muhammad cartoons is how the cartoons and the decision to publish them was seen by a different audience as a just and defensible action exercising the fundamental right to freedom of expression. In fact, it might be said, perhaps somewhat paradoxically, that the appropriation of the cartoons as an injustice symbol by some served as proof of their just nature for others. In a different twist on the audience dependent nature of injustice symbols, the same event/situation may become an injustice symbol for several audiences/collectives, but with highly divergent perspectives on interpretations, causes, and solutions. The Guantanamo Bay detention center, for example, is an injustice symbol for both al-Qaeda and Amnesty International (see chapter 3). While it would be hard to find many similarities between these two organizations, they do both see Guantanamo Bay as a symbol of the unjust nature of (parts of) the war against terrorism. Where they differ is on the root causes of the war and the kinds of actions that it legitimates.

The preceding section noted how injustice symbols are often part of symbolic families, that is, a group of symbols that reinforce and point to each other in a supportive and supplementary way. However, injustice symbols may also be related and mutually reinforcing in a much more conflictive manner. *Mutual production* occurs when one event/situation may be plausibly seen as part of a political response to another event/situation. This dynamic is probably most visible in political violence motivated by unjust events/situations. While the Abu Ghraib prisoner abuse became an injustice symbol in its own right, it is evident how this symbol cannot be separated from another major injustice symbol, the 9/11 attacks, which motivated the war against terrorism (see chapter 3). *Counter-symbolization* is typically a response to dominant injustice symbols contested and resisted by a collective. While the Holocaust is a globally shared (and dominant) injustice symbol and trauma (Alexander, 2004b), this interpretation is resisted by groups on the extreme Right in which, directly and indirectly, Adolf Hitler serves as a powerful counter-symbol or counter-icon, which is energized, as it were, by the dominant (Holocaust) symbol (see also chapter 6).

*Innocence*

As noted elsewhere, injustice symbols are a combination of object and meaning. Symbolization occurs when an object is imputed with universalizing meanings. This process, while essentially socially constructive, is never detached from empirical reality. Certain empirically grounded *determinants* are thus vital for the facilitation of symbol formation. The most important of these is victim *innocence*. Innocence has different shades. *Pure innocence* is at play when the victim(s) in an event/situation were more or less random victims of unjust exercise of authority. Consider, for example, the massacre perpetrated by American troops in 1968 at the Vietnamese village of My Lai. Soldiers were searching for Viet Cong operatives and Viet Cong supporters, but as the story broke (with considerable delay), it became apparent that the link between the Viet Cong and the victims was at best very weak. This was supported by the fact that numerous children were among those killed (Gray and Martin, 2008; Schlegel, 1995). The case of Khaled Said discussed earlier also exemplifies pure innocence when it emerged that the violence committed by police had no self-defensive purpose, and that Said had not committed any crime (Olesen, 2013b). *Qualified innocence* is at play when the victim(s) have engaged in activities that normally justify the exercise of authority, but where authority treatment and reaction is nevertheless seen as illegitimate, immoral, and/

or disproportionate. When the Abu Ghraib scandal, documented by photographs of wards humiliating prisoners, went public in 2004, the moral shock was not derived from presumed pure innocence on part of the prisoners but rather from legal and moral conceptions concerning the just treatment of prisoners irrespective of the question of guilt. Similarly, Nelson Mandela's imprisonment in apartheid South Africa did have a legal basis in his activities in the armed resistance against apartheid. Nevertheless, because the regime was seen as illegitimate and the armed struggle, hence, as a morally and politically defensible position (at least for some), the long-term prison sentence was considered both disproportionate and unjust, thus providing Mandela with an aura of (qualified) innocence. Of course, innocence, pure or qualified, is not an objective category but part of the contestation processes discussed above. The case of Khaled Said, used as an example of pure innocence, in fact demonstrates a movement from qualified to pure innocence. Under pressure, authorities did admit to some degree of police violence but maintained that this was justified in light of Said's "criminal" background and the circumstances surrounding his arrest. When these explanations were countered by witnesses, family, and friends, Said's innocence acquired increasing purity (Olesen, 2013b).

The perception of innocence is often amplified and supported through photographic documentation. Photographic documentation has a potential bearing on innocence in three ways. First, *in flagranti* photos or video capture an unjust act as it unfolds and thus provide evidence about the level and direction of aggression. This was the case, for example, in 1991 when a bystander with a video recorder documented disproportionally aggressive Los Angeles Police Department (LAPD) behavior toward a suspect, Rodney King (Alexander and Jacobs, 1998: 34–38; Martin, 2005). The beating quickly acquired symbolic status as it was increasingly portrayed by media and political activists as a symbol of systematic and institutionalized racism in the LAPD (the photos from Abu Ghraib also belong in this category) (see also Greer and McLaughlin, 2010). Second, *post-facto* photographs or video document the *consequences* of unjust behavior. Because such photos are taken post-facto, they do not contain the same kind of information about levels and directions of aggression as *in flagranti* documentation. Rather, the power of such photographs resides in their ability to generate emotional reactions (moral shocks) when viewers are faced with the vulnerability of human bodies (Alexander, Bartmanski, and Giesen, 2012; Butler, 2004; Sontag, 2003; Taylor, 1998; Zelizer, 2010). The photographs that emerged from the massacre at My Lai (see above) belong in this category. These photographs actually only became publicly known more than a year after the massacre. While the photos did not in and by themselves prove victim's innocence, the horrifying scenes with dead women and children huddled together became powerful resources for actors attempting to raise awareness and turn My Lai into an injustice symbol (Gray and Martin, 2008; Schlegel, 1995). Third, *pre-event* photographs are photographs of victims before they became victims (as such this category mainly involves individual victims). These are typically normal portraits or depict everyday situations involving the victim. When available, they are often circulated alongside photographs from the above categories. Like those in the second category, such photographs do not and cannot establish innocence by themselves. What they can do is to lend credibility and emotional information to claims about innocence and injustice. In the case of Neda Agha Soltan (see chapter 5), the grueling footage of Neda bleeding to death in the street were subsequently contrasted with pre-event photographs of a smiling, beautiful woman, the two sets of photographs dialectically infusing each other with injustice and innocence meaning (see also Olesen, 2013b, for a related observation on Khaled Said in Egypt).

GLOBALITY

The recent text discussed injustice symbols in a relatively general sense. Injustice symbols can be active at various spatial levels and sometimes confined to only one. The focus of this book, however, is on those injustice symbols that have a global dimension. A global injustice symbol has two main characteristics: its formation has involved actors from outside the local/national context of the originating event/situation; and it contains meanings for globally dispersed audiences in a global public sphere. The goal here is not to unpack all the complexities of this definition but to focus on three with particular relevance for the upcoming analyses: (a) the interaction between spatial levels and the different trajectories leading to the formation of global injustice symbols; (b) meaning change and adaptation; and (c) the role of media and communication networks.

*Spatial Levels and Trajectories*
The objects underlying injustice symbols are always local/national and particular in the sense that injustice happens to some*one* some*where*. Yet, in the contemporary world local/national events and situations are increasingly disembedded (Giddens, 1991) and involved in processes of scale shift (Bob, 2005; Olesen, 2005, 2007a, 2007b, 2009; Tarrow, 2005). We may distinguish between two ideal typical trajectories in the process of scale shift. In the *first*, which we may call the *step pattern*, global resonance is preceded by activities at the local/national level. During the Tunisian Revolution, Mohamed Bouazizi, who self-immolated as a protest against local authorities in December 2010 (see above), became a global injustice symbol of the harsh political and economic realities in many countries of the Arab world. Yet Bouazizi's global status only came after he had already acquired political status, first at the local level of his hometown of Sidi Bouzid, and, later, in January 2011, at a nationwide level (Olesen, 2013c). Similarly, the global resonance sparked by the violence against Malala Yousafzai and Jyoti Singh (see above) came on the back of significant protests in their respective countries. In some cases, in a dynamic resembling the so-called boomerang pattern (Keck and Sikkink, 1998), local/national actors may actively seek to globally promote the event/situation in order to activate pressure on local and national authorities (see also Bob, 2005). What this suggests is that the relationship between the local/national and global level is not a zero-sum game. Injustice symbols can be local, national, and global at the same time (see also chapter 6 for a critical discussion of this relationship). In the *second* trajectory, which we may label the *circumvention pattern*, the local/national level is bypassed, with the event/situation feeding more or less directly into the global public sphere and acquiring symbolic status primarily at this level. This pattern was evident in the case of

Neda Agha Soltan in Iran (see above and chapter 5) whose video-recorded death became globally available within minutes and hours. The circumvention pattern is often at play when local/national political conditions impede action and protest at this level or when local/national resources for action are only limitedly present. Neda's death, for example, could not be protested in Iran without severe repercussions. The circumvention pattern also includes a number of injustice symbols that have acquired significant status at the global level but for political reasons, not at the national level. The Srebrenica massacre on thousands of Bosnian Muslims by the Serb-Bosnian army under Ratko Mladic has, for example, become a core injustice symbol at a global (and especially European) level but remains controversial and contested in Serbia. Similar dynamics surround the Nanking massacre, 1937–1938, and the Armenian genocide, 1915–1918, which have attained only partial and contested injustice symbol status in the perpetrating countries: Japan and Turkey.

*Meaning Change and Adaptation*
Arguing that global injustice symbols may have meaning at various spatial levels and "belong" to a multiplicity of audiences in a global public sphere does not imply *meaning homogeneity*. On the contrary, we should expect the same symbols to be differently understood by different audiences. The theme of varying audience interpretation has been addressed already, but mainly from the point of diverging political-ideological orientations. A focus on geographically and culturally bound interpretations brings out another important dynamic: the potential simplification and *adaptation* process often involved when injustice symbols shift scale. As noted, global resonance and symbol formation occurs when actors outside the original spatial context adopt and critically engage with a local/national event or situation. But adoption and critical engagement always involves a degree of adaptation where the adopter construes the issue according to their *political-cultural schemas* (see above). In this way, and echoing what was said in the "Injustice Symbols and Society" section, global injustice symbols not only point to the victims and their context but they also say something important about the adopter and their moral

and political self-understanding (see chapters 2 and 5). Many global injustice symbols are based on events and situations outside of Europe and the United States but predominantly constructed by actors from within these regions. This suggests a certain regional bias in the formation of global injustice symbols and points to the dominance of Western-based political-cultural schemas in the global public sphere and at the level of global society (this topic is taken up for critical discussion in the book's concluding chapter 6).

*Media and Communication Networks*
The scale shifts involved in the formation of global injustice symbols depend on information and communication. The history of the modern world is in many ways the history of how technological developments have allowed for increasingly complex cross-spatial communication (Deibert, 1997; Thompson, 1995). The present, often hyperbolic, focus on new media technologies should not blind us to the fact that cross-spatial communication has always taken place, within, of course, the bounds of the available means of communication. Several of the injustice symbols mentioned at the beginning of the chapter were formed in a period without social media and Internet: for example, My Lai, Rodney King, and Nelson Mandela (see chapter 2). In these cases, communication mainly consisted of a combination of media accounts (both neutral and objective) and activist generated and distributed information. We can speak of this period as one characterized by *organized communication*. Yet it is appropriate to argue that with the acceleration of communication flows resulting from technological innovation (Castells, 2012), the conditions and potential for injustice symbol formation and preservation have expanded in at least four ways in the present period characterized by *networked communication*. First, at the most basic level, new technologies have made communication faster, cheaper, and easier. Second, and partly following from the above, the establishment of communication technologies, which are simultaneously individualized and networked, has created huge global citizen interfaces (Bennett and Segerberg, 2012). Third, digitalized communication and distribution

platforms such as, especially, YouTube serve as globally available *information and memory archives* where injustice symbols acquire permanent visibility for global audiences. Fourth, the development of portable and digitized documentation devices has facilitated citizen journalism (Allan and Thorsen, 2009; Greer and McLaughlin, 2010; Russell, 2011), that is, situations where bystanders, coincidentally or consciously, document events.

As indicated earlier, these developments are central in the pattern referred to as the circumvention pattern. Because of portable documentation devices and the ease and speed of digitized dissemination, information can easily escape the local/national level and feed into the communication flows of the global public sphere. This is advantageous under most conditions as it increases visibility and hence enhances the potential of resonance but is especially decisive under conditions where local/national authorities attempt to control communication. Given that the kind of information discussed here is often *visual*, these processes of scale shift are closely associated with the production of innocence through photographic documentation detailed above. For all the focus on new technologies, the reality is that they often interact with "old" media in scale shift and symbol formation. The early local protests in December 2010 inspired by Mohamed Bouazizi's self-immolation (see above) were video documented using cell phones by Ali Bouazizi, a cousin of Mohamed Bouazizi, and Rochdi Horchani, who participated in the protests alongside Mohamed Bouazizi's mother (Eko, 2012: 130; Ryan, 2011). The footage was uploaded to Facebook and from there it was picked up by Al-Jazeera's Mubasher channel, a news channel specializing in live and unedited airing of events, conferences, and debates (Eko, 2012: 130; Lim, 2013; Ryan, 2011; Schraeder and Redissi, 2011: 11). Only two days later, on December 19, the videos were uploaded to YouTube. These observations point to crucial *inter-media* dynamics. While news about Bouazizi and the protests in Sidi Bouzid was initially publicized via Facebook, they only gained wider attention, including outside Tunisia, when major pan-Arabian and global news channel Al-Jazeera started airing it.

GLOBAL SOCIAL MOVEMENTS

As argued in the "Injustice Symbols and Society" section, injustice symbols are a product of *moral-political* action. The focus on moral-political action is central to the understanding of the concept of social movements in the book (it is acknowledged though that not all forms of movement-related action can be meaningfully captured by this definition). What is argued in other words is that social movements should not be defined according to the type of actors but rather to the type of action. *Social movements are thus sequences (this may be both short and longer term) of moral-political action consisting of a combination and variety of actors who, verbally or visually, express indignation and dissatisfaction over a perceived injustice (the moral dimension), and issue calls for further mobilization and/or ameliorative action by systems of authority (the political dimension).* The specific combination of actors, as will be evident in the coming chapters, varies and is thus an analytical rather than theoretical question. For such social movements to qualify as *global*, the actors involved must come from several national contexts and/or be global in their composition (this is the case for international institutions and some activist organizations such as Amnesty International). The following briefly elaborates on the relevant actor categories employing a distinction between moral-political and professional-rational logics in their activities.

*Activists* are organized (the level of organization varies in terms of formalization and professionalization) citizens and/or professionals working on political issues and change outside the channels of political parties and interest organizations. The moral-political logic is dominant for these kinds of actors, although activists and their organizations obviously also make decisions based on a professional-rational logic (e.g., Bob, 2005). Some actors within the activist category may have a more individualized character: for example, artists and priests working with a clearly activist agenda. The *media's* involvement in the formation and employment of injustice symbols primarily resides in the latter's correspondence with established news criteria such as conflict, drama, and personalization (e.g., Bennett, 1983/2005). This is not to suggest that the media do not also act for moral-political reasons; in general, they see themselves as playing a critical and democratic role in society (Alexander, 2006; Strömbäck, 2005). When the media is involved in injustice symbol formation and employment, we often find the professional-rational and moral-political logics to combine. *Politicians and political parties* are expected by the media and the electorate to relate to instances of violence and potential injustice, including those outside their national context (such expectations obviously vary across the political spectrum, e.g., an extreme rightwing party will generally not be expected by its electorate to react to instances of distant suffering). As in the case of the media, this does not imply that they only act based on a professional-rational logic of environment expectations. When politicians and/or political parties become centrally involved in the formation and employment of injustice symbols, we typically see an intersection of the two logics. Whether or not *states* become engaged in the formation and employment of injustice symbols depends on a variety of factors such as government "color," historical context, and geopolitical interests (e.g., a state may be especially inclined to get involved if events can serve to delegitimize another state with which it has a conflictive relationship). As is evident, the professional-rational and moral-political logics play varying roles in these factors. Although realists in international relations (IR) contend that strategic action is predominant in state behavior, constructivist and institutionalist strands in IR have convincingly shown how state behavior also has a moral-political dimension (e.g., Keck and Sikkink, 1998; Klotz, 1995; Lumsdaine, 1993). *International institutions* are the creations of states, but as thoroughly demonstrated by institutionalist and regime scholars within IR, such institutions develop rationales and worldviews that are at least partly independent from the states that undergird them. The UN is of particular interest in the context of global injustice symbols as this institution was founded on a moral-political basis and continues to see its global role in this light. *Networked citizens* have a resemblance with activists but differ from them in that the latter are typically organized at some level (see above). Highlighting networked citizens as political actors in their own right rests on the way communication technologies have developed in recent decades to allow political engagement in an increasingly individualized and mediated sense (Bennett and Segerberg, 2012; Castells, 2012). As is the case with activists, the activities of networked citizens are founded primarily on a moral-political logic.

## METHODOLOGY AND APPROACH

The specific methods and data collection strategies are detailed in the case chapters. The following offers some considerations on the general methodology and approach of the book. In overall terms, this can be characterized as *grounded, interpretive, selective*, and *dialectical*.

The theoretical and conceptual framework developed in the present chapter has emerged in a manner that reflects the *grounded theory* tradition (Glaser and Strauss, 1967)—that is, through empirical analysis. While the framework clearly draws on already existing theories and concepts, no whole or partial theory and conceptual vocabulary for injustice symbols are available in the sociological literature. The research process thus started with some rough theoretical and conceptual guides that were applied to a variety of empirical phenomena. These early analyses helped expand the theoretical and conceptual framework, which was then employed in the study of new cases and so on. The framework presented here has not, however, been developed solely on the cases studied in chapters 2–5. Thus, a number of other smaller or larger case studies not fully reported in the book were undertaken during the research process in order to increase density and credibility of the theoretical and conceptual framework. Many of these are illustratively referred to above. They include, most notably, Khaled Said (Olesen, 2013b), Mohamed Bouazizi (Olesen, 2013c), the Muhammad cartoons (Olesen, 2014), Mohamed al-Durrah, Rigoberta Menchú, Malala Yousafzai, and Jyoti Singh. As a result, all the case study chapters make an effort to show how the perspective of the chapter can be extended to other empirical cases.

As the preceding discussions have amply demonstrated, symbols are human constructs: they only exist in and through the meanings human actors impute to the underlying object. As a result the analyses in the book concentrate on the *interpretation* of this political meaning work (including the significant contestation and conflict such work often entails). Because meaning imputation is largely a linguistic process, the book's analyses focus strongly on human communication. The latter term is understood broadly as encompassing not only speech and writing but also various forms of artistic and photographic expression and documentation. An interpretive approach is not a retreat into the realm of the anecdotal, literary, or journalistic. The goal of the interpretive strategy adopted here is thus to *uncover patterns* and to make *causal arguments* about the relationship between actors, contexts, and symbols. The term "causal" is not used in the strictest sense in which some independent variable more or less mechanically causes something in the social and political world. A causal argument as understood here concerns the analytical and empirically grounded establishment of *relationships* between human actors/action and certain phenomena and outcomes. So, when it is argued in chapter 5 that the footage of the dying Neda Agha Soltan acquired added injustice meaning by being juxtaposed with photographs of Neda before she died, this is a causal argument. Similarly, when it is contended in chapter 4 that public expressions of regret by major figures such as Kofi Annan and Bill Clinton over the lack of intervention during the 1994 Rwandan genocide were central to establishing it as a global injustice symbol, it is a causal argument.

An interpretive approach must necessarily be *selective* (and even reductive). As noted by Alexander (2010: 294–295) the interpretation of human meaning work is always an exercise in reconstruction and complexity reduction. Symbolic processes involve a wide variety of actors and collectives and often occur over longer periods of time in which there is rarely any specific starting or end point. The researcher therefore needs to make a range of clearly articulated methodological choices and to consider their implications for the kinds of analyses that can be conducted and the conclusions that can be drawn. First, it is pertinent to specify which actors (see the "Global Social Movements" subsection) are studied (and which are not). For example, in chapter 3 on Guantanamo Bay, the focus is primarily on al-Qaeda's meaning work even if this organization is obviously not the only one to have engaged in such work. Second, while the meaning work surrounding injustice symbols may be carried out by certain actors, this process is intimately related to wider collectives or audiences. Since varieties of collectives/audiences are typically engaged in the symbolic process, we need to carefully outline precisely which the analysis focuses on. In chapter 5 on Neda Agha Soltan, for example, interest concerns the way she was adapted to resonate with a Western audience. Third, symbolic processes are precisely that: processes with no clear starting and end points. It should therefore be transparent at the outset where the analyst enters and leaves the process. This exercise may often involve selecting certain key moments that are then subjected to closer analysis. In chapter 2 on Nelson Mandela, a number of decisive moments are singled out in order to structure an analysis spanning a period of more than 50 years.

The emphasis above on human meaning work in the symbolic process does not imply a methodological move away from structure and context. This observation clearly reflects the overall theoretical argument (see figure 1.1) that symbol formation and employment should always be understood in relation to socially existing political-cultural schemas. This relationship is *dialectical*: injustice symbols are shaped through schemas, yet at the same time shape and expand them. This dialectical relationship should also be heeded methodologically. While the center of analysis is the meaning work surrounding injustice symbols, this should always be contextualized. Methodologically, contextualization implies attention to if and how actors, directly or indirectly, refer to the following: (a) already existing value and belief systems; (b) to other (injustice) symbols; or (c) to previous events and situations. Methodologically speaking, a dialectical approach involves constant analytical movement between these levels.

### PLAN OF THE BOOK

Apart from the present chapter, the book consists of four case study chapters (2–5) and a concluding chapter (6). All the case study chapters reflect on the book's core concepts and their relationships: global injustice symbols, global social movements, and global society (see figure 1.1).

The book opens with a chapter on *global political iconography* and an empirical focus on Nelson Mandela. The core theoretical idea is that icon formation always occurs in interplay between three elements: the empirical person's biography, agents, and audience. The underlying component for any iconic process is the exemplary life or biography. Yet this material needs to be developed and dramatized by political agents. For iconicity to develop on a larger scale, their work in turn must resonate with a wider audience, who accepts the icon as the embodiment of cherished values. Structured by these theoretical insights, the chapter offers a chronologically structured three-step analysis of formation, climax, and establishment in the global iconic process of Nelson Mandela. The chapter focuses on the role of the global antiapartheid movement in this process. A key finding of the chapter is how the celebration of Mandela is also a celebration of global society and its role in the freeing of Mandela and the collapse of apartheid.

Chapter 3 analyses the role of injustice symbols in the constitution of a *global grievance community* anchored in political Islam. The empirical focus is on the way the detention center at Guantanamo Bay has been constructed by al-Qaeda as a major global injustice symbol. The chapter analyzes al-Qaeda's discursive use of Guantanamo to expose moral corruption and hypocrisy on part of its creators, the United States. Guantanamo is considered to be part of a wider injustice hierarchy in which Guantanamo symbolizes the West's unjust and historically continuous aggression toward Muslims. It is shown, in continuation, how Guantanamo is anchored in a symbolic family, which includes events and situations such as Palestine, the Satanic Verses, and the Muhammad cartoons. The chapter discusses the contested nature of the Guantanamo Bay at a global level, including how actors working from radically different perspectives, such as Amnesty International, also view it as an injustice symbol related to the war against terrorism.

Chapter 4 argues and demonstrates that within a relatively short span of time, and culminating with the tenth anniversary in 2004, the 1994 Rwandan genocide has become a key *global injustice memory.* At the core of this process is a double-sided conception of injustice: on the one hand, the genocide in itself clearly constitutes a major injustice; on the other hand, injustice claims have been expanded to encompass actors outside of Rwanda who observed the horrors without instigating sufficient action to halt or at least mitigate the effects of the unfolding genocide. It is the fact that moral and political responsibility for the genocide has been so powerfully expanded to third parties in a spectatorship position that most vividly testifies to the global character of the Rwandan injustice memory. The chapter identifies and analyzes four areas in which the transformation of the Rwandan genocide from national event to global injustice memory has occurred: institutionalization, expressions of regret, analogical bridging, and cultural products.

Chapter 5 analyses the case of Neda Agha Soltan from a *dramatic diffusion* perspective. Through the graphic and immediately circulated images of her death during protests in Iran in 2009, Neda reached the global public sphere in a more or less unfiltered form. The analysis demonstrates how this basic component was transformed into a global injustice symbol through a globally available political-cultural schema contrasting Iran and the West. This schema is constituted by a number of dichotomous themes: religious-secular; oppression/ control-freedom; democratic-nondemocratic; and rational-irrational. The operation of the themes is visible on at least four levels: first, Neda and her death was placed in a wider historic and global struggle for democracy and human rights in which Iran was cast as a negative other; second, the package was confirmed by the Iranian regime itself as it denied any responsibility for Neda's death and even tried to blame it on non-Iranian actors such as the Central Intelligence Agency (CIA) and Western journalists; third, certain character traits were highlighted to portray Neda as innocent and as a victim of Islamic Iran (this involved emphasizing her relevance for women's rights); and fourth, these traits were supported by the circulation of pre-death photographs (showing a beautiful, young, smiling Neda). The concluding chapter 6 does four things. First, it summarizes the main findings of the individual case chapters. Second, it discusses the extent to which the case studies provide evidence of a global society. Third, it builds on these insights to expand and qualify the concept of the global civil sphere. Four, it concludes by summarizing the lessons of the book for the study of global social movements.

# CHAPTER 2

# POLITICAL ICONOGRAPHY

WHEN NELSON MANDELA, DEFYING FAILING HEALTH AND THE LOSS of his great-granddaughter only weeks earlier, attended the final and closing ceremony at the football 2010 World Cup in South Africa, he was greeted with standing ovation and worldwide media attention. His appearance despite personal hardships perfectly illustrated a political career spanning more than 60 years. During that time, Mandela suffered personal loss, repression, and prolonged imprisonment only to emerge as a moral and political victor when South African apartheid collapsed in the late 1980s and early 1990s. After this event, Mandela more or less disappeared from public life. News about him increasingly focused on serious health problems. When the world learned about his death, at the age of 95, on December 5, 2013, it hardly came as a surprise. Nevertheless, communicative networks immediately went red hot and filled the global public sphere with statements that were more or less unanimous in their praise of the man's accomplishments and significance. Despite being out of formal political circulation for almost 15 years (Mandela left office after 5 years as the first black president of South Africa in 1999), Mandela thus keeps stirring our global collective imagination. This concern with Mandela cuts across Left-Right political divides and geographic differences and animates politicians, activists, celebrities, and "ordinary" people alike. Mandela, it seems, has come to embody a range of human qualities and political-cultural values such as solidarity, reconciliation, democracy, and human rights for global audiences: he is, in other words, a global political icon (see various chapters in Barnard's, 2014, edited collection on Mandela).

Studying Mandela's iconicity contributes to our understanding of political symbols as outcomes (see chapter 1) of global social movement activities. There is wide agreement that global social movement action, outlined in chapter 1 in a broad sense, was central in the collapse of apartheid (e.g., Klotz, 1995; Thörn, 2006). This was indeed the core goal of the global antiapartheid movement. Yet, this movement also created other outcomes that can only be grasped and appreciated through a political-cultural and sociological lens. Mandela, the global icon, is perhaps the most important. The Mandela case in some ways pushes against the boundaries of the book's core term: "injustice symbols." While it is evident that Mandela, the icon, rests on shared notions of injustice, the meanings associated with him also display a strong sense of justice. This is so because the injustice suffered by Mandela was eventually fought and set right (in contrast to the book's other cases); an outcome accomplished, at least partly, by the global antiapartheid movement. The indisputable injustice surrounding Mandela's life consequently blends with the notion that it was the concerted and collective effort of individuals and organizations from all over the world that helped achieve final justice for Mandela and his fellow South Africans. As theorized in chapter 1, injustice symbol formation is thus a process that reflects not only on the object (in this case Mandela) underlying the symbol but also, to a considerable degree, on the audience and actors that construct the symbol or icon (this theme is addressed in more detail in the following analysis). The objective of this chapter is to map and analyze the process and transformation underlying Mandela's iconic status. It does so in three tempi: first, it looks at Mandela's time in prison (1962–1990) and considers how the iconic process was able to proceed despite Mandela's public absence; second, it is argued that the period from approximately 1988 to 1994 constituted the climax of his icon formation; and third, it discusses the extent to which his iconic status has "survived" and acquired stability beyond the time and events that originally placed him on the global scene. The conclusion discusses Mandela's iconicity from a critical perspective and in relation to global society.

## GLOBAL POLITICAL ICONOGRAPHY

This section offers a theoretical and conceptual treatment of global political iconography. It consists of two main subsections: the first provides a working definition of the concept of global political icon and the second outlines and develops the core theoretical elements of global political iconography. It is argued that the iconic process involves a combination of biography, agency, and audience/context.

### DEFINITION AND DELIMITATION

The core concept of global political icon may usefully be broken down into its three parts. It makes sense to start with the last element: "icon." This term has several meanings and usages in research and popular culture. Its employment here seeks to capture three dimensions in particular. First, icon literally means image. While the icons analyzed within this framework cannot be reduced to their visual representation, their personalized nature means that the visual aspect does play a central role. Second, icon refers to an image or person that embodies and symbolizes a period, an event, or a set of values. This is the core meaning of the term as it is used here. Third, the term has certain religious connotations. The argument is not that icons are religious per se but that the values associated with them often resonate with deep political-cultural and, in some instances, religious themes. *Global* political icons are icons that have acquired meaning for audiences in several national contexts. A qualification applies here. To say that an icon means something to people in different national settings does not imply meaning homogeneity; that is, the icon means the same to everyone familiar with it. Typically, the meanings associated with an icon will vary from one context to the next, reflecting nationally and regionally based political values. Global *political* icons are icons with clear political meanings. The adjective "political" is, above all, an attempt to separate this category from cultural icons such as Michael Jackson or Andy Warhol (in popular usage the term "icon" is typically reserved for personalities of this kind).

Icons can obviously be political in different ways. For example, Osama bin Laden, Che Guevara, as well as Nelson Mandela qualify as global political icons. These share certain traits but also differ in significant ways. Some of this difference can be understood via Alexander's (e.g., 2011) concept of moral binaries (see chapter 1). Some of the main values associated with Mandela are flexibility, forgiveness, and democracy. Icons such as bin Laden and Guevara are typically defined in more or less opposing terms, that is, are seen as inflexible, aggressive, and undemocratic. Of course, as suggested above, the meanings ascribed to icons are always group and audience dependent, thus suggesting that the values just outlined are neither fixed nor objective. The point here is rather to indicate how such icons are differently understood, via some of the binaries mentioned above, from within the same audience perspective and value/meaning universe. The theoretical framework of this chapter, while relevant for other types of icons, is primarily developed in relation to democratic- and rights-oriented icons (including figures such as Aung San Suu Kyi, Malala Yousafzai, Dalai Lama, Martin Luther King, and Mahatma Gandhi).

## CORE CONCEPTUAL AND THEORETICAL ELEMENTS

The struggle that the background person (this term will be applied in order to be able to make an analytical distinction between the "empirical" person and the symbolically laden and iconized person) comes to symbolize in the process of political iconography is typically about the granting of rights and democratic freedom to a collective. This requires taking the moral-political high ground by claiming that an intolerable injustice is being committed against a more or less well-defined collective by specified violators. If a person purporting to struggle on behalf of such moral and collective ideas can be shown to act immorally (e.g., by lying or dramatizing the truth) or in a self-interested manner (e.g., by amassing personal wealth), the iconic process is distorted.[1] Religious saints are real people who are elevated to a quasi-divine level. Secular icons, in a somewhat similar manner, are thus expected to rise above the mundane and "dirty" world of politics. What is peculiar about the iconic process, however, is that in parallel with this moral elevation of the icon's personal and political life there is often a pronounced concern with his or her humanness and imperfection. In fact, it seems that the successful iconic process requires a certain humbleness and even resistance to it. A person considered to be actively seeking iconic status will immediately raise suspicions about self-interested behavior that conflict with the conception and expectation of moral purity. This underlines a central tension in the iconic process. On the one hand, it revolves around an outstanding individual with an exemplary biography. On the other hand, that individual must in a sense "hide" him- or herself and actively work to integrate his/her individuality in a collective moral-political vision: the individual is universalized. This merging of the individual and the collective is achieved, for example, by the icon's acknowledgment that his/her special status has been awarded him or her by others and ultimately builds on the efforts of those others.

What sets icons apart from "normal" political actors is the example and drama of their lives. Personal sacrifice is a central element in this drama. So strong is their commitment to the pursuit of justice that they are willing to risk life and health and largely abandon ordinary family and career patterns. The sacrificial aspect facilitates the inscription of moral purity because it underlines the profound commitment to values that are in a sense above the individual. Through sacrifice, the person comes to be seen as an instrument for a higher cause; the individual is erased and a personae or symbol emerges. Juergensmeyer (1987: 198) describes something similar in Gandhi's transformation to what he calls a modern saint. For his admirers, Gandhi's renouncement of personal wealth and comfort in the context of political struggle made him an almost Christlike figure. Even if the political icons in focus in this chapter are secular icons, the notions of moral purity, personal sacrifice, and moral strength/physical weakness has certain religious roots in the exemplary life and suffering of Christ. It is also, as shown by Campbell (1949), a recurrent theme in fairytales and religious narratives across cultures. The hero is typically someone who undertakes a journey full of ordeals and in the end returns triumphantly with new powers to restore and/or recreate society. In modern secular iconization, these ordeals can have various forms: for example, Gandhi's renunciation of physical comfort and pleasures,

Aung San Suu Kyi's and Nelson Mandela's prolonged imprisonments, and Malala Yousafzai's near death when she was shot by the Taliban in 2012 for advocating the right of education for girls. In the case of modern and secular iconicity, these sacrifices are always made on behalf of a specified set of political values and principles, that is, the person faces ordeals in defense of some religious or political value set. These ordeals and sacrifices and the willingness to face them bestows the individual with new moral-political powers that grant them the authority to speak for and represent the values they defend.

In most cases, the background person has been a victim of state repression. When the repressive apparatus of the state is set in motion, the individual is easily crushed or otherwise affected in life-changing ways. This bodily and personal weakness vis-à-vis a powerful state is contrasted with the moral strength of the icon. In fact, there is a dialectical relationship between the two where moral strength seems to increase almost exponentially with the level of repression (Alexander, 2006, 2011; Hess and Martin, 2006; McAdam, 2000).[2] First, the power and violence unleashed by the state is proof to the audience that the struggle matters. Second, the use of force within such a moral-political context is, or can be interpreted as, a display of impotence. The power of the perpetrator is, in a sense, morally transferred to the victim. Often icons display the impotence and immoral character of the oppressive state by refraining from violence themselves and even by pleading forgiveness for present or former oppressors. In fact, the renunciation of violence is often central to the type of political icons treated here, and distinguishes them from revolutionary and militant icons (see the "Definition and Delimitation" subsection above). Again, this kind of political icon invokes a lineage with roots in the life of Christ, but one which in recent history has attained a more political character with Mohandas Gandhi and, later, Martin Luther King (as shown by Alexander, 2006, and Chabot and Duyvendak, 2002, Gandhi's nonviolence strategy was a key inspiration in the American civil rights movement).

As shown above, iconicity is dependent on biography, on certain values, goals, and characteristics expressed in observable behavior and action. Yet iconicity does not arise more or less automatically from the exemplary life. The exemplary life may provide the necessary elements for the iconic process but the latter requires that the exemplary life is recognized, publicized, and dramatized by agents with moral-political interests and/or involvement in the struggle that the icon is considered to represent. In the case of global political iconography, such agents must display a degree of national and regional spread. In this context, agency is typically a form of solidarity agency. The background person of the iconic process is always tied to a specific place and a specific political struggle. He or she is a national actor globalized by agents from without these borders. Agents of this kind are not directly involved in the political struggle but relate to it in a solidaristic and moral-political sense. Since political icon formation is about the bestowal of moral and political values, the meaning work of agents always takes place in an interaction with audience and political context. In fact, we can think of solidarity agents as mediators between the background person and the values and value expectations of an audience in a given historical setting (Kane, 2001: 33, makes a related observation when he notes how the moral capital of political leaders is always intimately tied to the values of a specific audience or constituency). The agency-driven relationship between political icon and audience underlines a point made earlier that political icons are essentially socialized and universalized individuals. In his analysis of Abraham Lincoln in collective American memory, Schwartz (1990) dissects how Lincoln memories have significantly changed over time and in ways clearly shaped by audience expectations and political-cultural context. In explaining the increasing popularity of Lincoln in the early twentieth century, he notes (101), "Lincoln was not elevated at this time because the people had discovered new facts about him, but because they had discovered new facts about themselves, and regarded him as the perfect vehicle for giving these tangible expression." This is an essentially Durkheimian point: symbols and icons are social constructs that condense the values and self-understandings of a collective in a given spatiotemporal context (see chapter 1). This argument has several implications for the study of global political icons: first, it suggests that in trying to understand why certain persons attain iconic status, we need to clearly situate them in the global political context they emerge in; and second, it indicates that the iconic process not only involves who the icon is but also equally who the global audiences infusing him or her with moral-political meaning are and aspire to be.

## NELSON MANDELA AND ANTIAPARTHEID

The following offers a three-step analysis of Mandela's transformation to global political icon. The first discusses how icon formation was able to evolve during Mandela's prison years (1962–1990). The second demonstrates how Mandela's global iconicity climaxed from 1988 to 1994. The third shows and argues that Mandela is now a firmly established and recognized global icon. Building on the theoretical framework, emphasis in the analysis will be on the interaction between icon/biography, agents, and audience.

### A Note on Data and Approach

The study of political iconography presents several methodological challenges. Iconic processes are precisely that—processes without clearly identifiable points of beginning or ending. Nevertheless, the task of sociological analysis is to identify and uncover key moments, events, and actions in the processes and to locate them in their political context. Such an approach necessarily involves a good deal of reduction and selection. This is particularly marked in the case of Mandela whose political career spans a period of more than 60 years. A significant part of the research has thus consisted in identifying key moments, events, and actions. To acquire the necessary overview for making these research decisions, two types of sources were consulted in the initial phase: first, as will be shown later, Mandela biographies and autobiographies are extremely numerous and provide an immensely rich material for analysis in their own right; and second, there is a good amount of academic literature on the antiapartheid movement, which offers insights into the development of Mandela's iconicity (several of these works are referred to below). Key moments, events, and actions selected for closer analysis are the following: The Rivonia Trials in 1964, Mandela's sixtieth birthday in 1978 and the solidarity activities surrounding this event, the 1988 Nelson Mandela 70th Birthday Tribute concert at Wembley, the release of Mandela from prison on February 11, 1990, the 1990 concert celebrating his freedom (also at Wembley), and the awarding of the Nobel Peace Prize in 1993 (with Willem de Klerk). In analyzing these events, two types of empirical material have been central. First, speeches, documents, and actions by Mandela have been scrutinized with an emphasis on the way they facilitated the iconic process. In particular, attention is given to those places where Mandela outlines his own role in the antiapartheid struggle and his relationship with solidarity agents in and outside of South Africa. Second, focus is on the way solidarity and other agents portray and interpret Mandela and, not least, what kinds of actions they have engaged in to publicize his achievements. These two lines of inquiry reflect the theoretical argument made above: iconicity results from an interaction between icon/biography, agents, and audience.

In terms of geography, the analysis highlights aspects of iconization within a European context, and especially within the United Kingdom, which was perhaps the core of global solidarity activities. This is an admittedly reductive choice, as Mandela's appeal cannot obviously be confined to any one country or region. However, given the historical scope of the analysis, it was necessary to center analysis only on certain moments as well as on selected countries and regions.

BACKGROUND

Mandela the icon is tied to the historical experience of the apartheid system in South Africa. This system was implemented from 1948 onward when the National Party gained political power in South Africa. The apartheid system had deep roots in South Africa's colonial past and divided the population into four main categories: white, black, colored, and Indian. This division served as the basis of several segregationist policies, including the forced removal of millions of people into designated areas centered round racial characteristics and voting reforms that effectively reduced voting rights to the white population. Apartheid was met with growing internal opposition from

the disenfranchised majority of South Africa. Several political organizations representing blacks, coloreds, and Indians had emerged in
the first part of the twentieth century in response to racial and colonial inequalities, most notably the ANC (African National Congress,
1923) and the SACP (South African Communist Party, 1921). In the
second half of the century, and partly motivated by the implementation of apartheid, a new wave of organizations emerged such the
PAC (Pan Africanist Congress of Azania, 1959) and the IFP (Inkatha
Freedom Party, 1975). The resistance against apartheid started gaining increasing global attention from the 1950s onward, at first mainly
within the context of the Commonwealth, but gradually expanding
to most Western European countries and the United States. Nelson
Mandela was born in 1918 into a family with royal status. In the
1940s Mandela studied law in Johannesburg where he became part of
the ANC and the ANC Youth League and quickly acquired a leadership position. During the late 1950s and early 1960s, inspired by the
Sharpeville massacre and armed resistance movements in the Third
World, Mandela advocated armed resistance against apartheid. It was
in this context that he was arrested in 1962.

PRISON AND ICON FORMATION

Nelson Mandela spent almost 28 years in prison (1962–1990). When
he disappeared into this enforced exile, Mandela was already a well-
known figure in antiapartheid circles, especially at the national level,
but nowhere near the iconic and popular status that he would later
achieve. One might think that being removed from political life in
this manner would have had an adverse effect on icon formation (evidently, this was what apartheid authorities had hoped to achieve). Yet,
despite these apparently obstructive conditions, Mandela's iconic status kept developing, if only slowly, during the following decades. To
understand this paradox four factors need highlighting: (1) the symbolic power of prison; (2) prior reputation; (3) isolation and mythol-
ogy; and (4) global agency and attention.
　　Imprisonment has important symbolic potential. Presupposing
that the struggle leading to imprisonment already has some public

standing, prison can become a symbolic center for that struggle (for the related case of Guantanamo Bay, see Olesen, 2011). Imprisonment is always a highly visible act of power on the part of authorities. To be considered legitimate, it must be firmly grounded on evidence and appear apolitical. The conviction of Mandela and other ANC activists in 1964 at the so-called Rivonia trials did not meet any of these criteria.[3] It was widely seen, in as well as outside of South Africa, as an attempt to silence opposition and cut off the heads of the burgeoning antiapartheid movement in South Africa. Under these conditions, imprisonment immediately attained two symbolic meanings. First, it became evidence of the very injustice that antiapartheid activists were fighting. While imprisonment put an end to certain organizational and political activities, it backfired (Hess and Martin, 2006) by enhancing the moral stature of those imprisoned. Second, imprisonment could be interpreted as a sign of weakness on the part of those employing it. It signaled that the struggle was beginning to be a significant cause of worry for authorities.

Mandela's icon formation was able to develop during imprisonment only because the foundations for it had already been laid. Mandela, says biographer Anthony Sampson (1999: 199), "went to jail with all the glory of a lost leader, in an aura of martyrdom." Before his arrest in 1962, Mandela had thus established himself as a key leader of the ANC and its armed branch Umkhonto we Sizwe (see endnote 3). During this time he achieved popular status and became known as the Black Pimpernel because of his ability to evade attempts to capture him, often traveling incognito around the country. And once caught Mandela did not go silently to prison. Despite the evidently political nature of the Rivonia trial, it was no mere show trial; it provided Mandela and other activists with the right to defend themselves and, as such, with a public platform. Most notably, Mandela's (1964) four-hour speech from the dock on April 20, 1964, became a powerful resource in the iconic process to come. The final sentences in particular came to reverberate and define the character of Mandela: "During my lifetime I have dedicated myself to this struggle of the African people...I have cherished the ideal of a democratic and free society...It is an ideal, which I hope to live for and to achieve. But if needs be, it is an ideal for which I am prepared to die."[4]

Mandela's speech and apparent readiness to make the ultimate sacrifice for the cause set him above mundane politics. "Common" politicians and activists may be highly committed to their political concerns but few will accept death as a possible consequence and hold so strongly to their ideals in a situation of imminent danger. That Mandela's words were not just rhetorical bravado has been accounted for later by lawyers and fellow activists who tried to change Mandela's mind about the final parts of the speech, fearing that it would be taken by authorities as a provocation they would need to react on (Maclennan, 2010). With the speech, Mandela not only set himself apart from the ordinary world of politics but he also distinguished himself from the rest of the prisoners sentenced at the Rivonia trial. The speech gave him a unique cache of moral-political status and capital to be drawn on and developed over the coming decades.

Perhaps paradoxically, prison life provided optimum conditions for this process. Being imprisoned also isolates you from the mundane world of politics, with difficult decisions, political infighting, criticism, and personal and political mistakes. In prison Mandela could, in a certain sense, do nothing wrong. Rather, and facilitated by the Rivonia trial speech and the status he had already attained, his reputation as a key moral-political figure was allowed to grow unhindered by the constant pitfalls of active political life. More or less incommunicado, nor could Mandela resist (that is not to say that he would) his transformation into the key symbol of the antiapartheid struggle. In the isolation of prison, Mandela was a human "material" that could be shaped into the desired symbolic form. And as time went by, and with limited information coming out of Robben Island, Mandela gradually attained semi-mythological status (Tomaselli and Boster, 1993: 7).

While Mandela's isolation, as well as the other factors outlined above, may have facilitated his icon formation, they cannot explain it. The background person of the iconic process and the events and conditions surrounding him or her thus provides certain resources for the iconic process, but this biographic material has to be embraced, molded, interpreted, and dramatized by actors politically related to or sympathetic to the background person and his/her struggle. This work was carried out by the global antiapartheid solidarity movement that began emerging in the 1950s and early 1960s (e.g., Culverson, 1996; Fieldhouse, 2005; Gurney, 2000; Klein, 2009; Klotz, 1995; Sanders, 2000; Skinner, 2009; Stultz, 1991; Thörn, 2006, 2009). The primary horizon of meaning for the global antiapartheid movement was the issue of racial inequality and colonization (for some organizations and activists this theme had religious roots, while others cast it mainly in secular-political terms), which, with the process of decolonization and the American civil rights movement, had gained new prominence in the decades after World War II. The injustice iconization of Mandela was thus built on a well-defined and globally available *political-cultural schema* and a set of binaries that increasingly defined racial inequality and racially motivated repression as antisocial and antidemocratic.

Global antiapartheid was obviously not focused primarily on Mandela but on apartheid as a whole. As noted by Reddy (personal correspondence), Albert Luthuli, president of the ANC from 1952 to 1960 and the first African to receive the Nobel Peace Prize (1960), was a prominent figure during the early years. Yet from the mid-1970s, a strategy began to take shape in which Mandela would gradually become its symbolic center. The ten-year period between the Rivonia trial and the mid-1970s was relatively quiet: after a spate of public attention in 1964, Mandela and the other prisoners seemed to retreat into the shadows (Sampson, 1999: 259). Yet they were not completely forgotten, and important groundwork for the next phase was laid during this period.[5] Ruth First's edited collection of Mandela articles and addresses, first published in 1965 in a direct response to the Rivonia trial, provided crucial background information for the early stages of antiapartheid activism and, not least importantly, served to make Mandela a focal point in it. The forewords by the editor and Oliver Tambo (then leader of the ANC) drew the contours of an individual with special qualities and destined to lead the struggle against apartheid:

> Mandela, it is whispered through prison walls, is as magnetic a political prisoner as he was once mass orator and underground political commander and he continues to radiate the confidence, the strength

and the moral authority that has sustained the African freedom struggle in its most difficult days; and that will, in time, bring the apartheid system toppling down. (First, 1965/1973: vii)

Fellow ANC activist Oliver Tambo was equally eulogistic in his characterization:

> He has a natural air of authority. He cannot help magnetizing a crowd...He is dedicated and fearless. He is the born mass leader...He is unrelenting, yet capable of flexibility and delicate judgment. He is an outstanding individual, but he knows that he derives his strength from the great masses of people who make up the freedom struggle in our country. (Tambo, 1965/1973: xi–xiii)

Thus, while the period from 1964 to the mid-1970s was perhaps rather low-intensive in relation to Mandela and the other prisoners at Robben Island, certain actors and activities served to keep them in the global public eye. Yet Mandela was still not near the same level of popularization that he would achieve from the mid-1970s. The beginning of this crucial phase was centered round Mandela's approaching sixtieth birthday in 1978.[6] Accounts by key activists of the time indicate that the acceleration of Mandela's iconicity was largely a strategic decision (Kane, 2001: 129). Enuga S. Reddy, a leading official in the UN Special Committee on Apartheid (see also Thörn, 2006: 31–33), recalls how decisions were made in 1976–1977 to place Mandela as the figurehead of the antiapartheid struggle:

> Now my idea was not only to do something for Mandela but for the other prisoners also, but I talked to Oliver Tambo and he said, no, keep to Mandela, he was a symbol, you see, because some people wanted to honor Oliver Tambo, but he didn't want that, so it became focused on Mandela, so Mandela before that was a prominent leader...but after that he became the symbol of the struggle, it was built up. (Interview conducted by Håkan Thörn on June 19, 2000, in New York)[7]

Mandela's birthday thus "rang around the world...From Britain, antiapartheid campaigners sent ten thousand birthday cards (which never arrived)" (Sampson, 1999: 296). The birthday campaign propelled

Mandela into a new and popularized iconic phase. The success of the campaign, according to Klein (2009: 466), "rested largely on the fact that it was able to attract supporters from different political persuasions, those not politically aware, and the youth." The Mandela cause was increasingly embraced by individuals and organizations outside the immediate circle of antiapartheid activism. By 1978, Mandela was thus beginning the transformation that, over the next decade, would turn him into a global household name (see the next subsection, "Freedom and Iconic Climax," on the iconic climax in the 1988–1994 period).

In 1978, British-based International Defence and Aid Fund for Southern Africa published a major compilation of Mandela speeches and writings "brought together to mark his 60th birthday" (International Defence and Aid Fund for Southern Africa, 1978). A notable element of that book was an interview with S. R. "Mac" Maharaj. Maharaj was sentenced alongside Mandela at the Rivonia trial in 1964 and served 12 years at Robben Island. When he was released in 1976, he brought with him new information about conditions on the island as well as new "material" for the formation of Mandela's iconicity. While previous accounts (see, e.g., First, 1965/1973; and Tambo, 1965/1973) had portrayed Mandela as a powerful and dedicated revolutionary leader and militant, Maharaj's recollections offered glimpses of a more balanced and less intransigent Mandela; a man changed by his many years in prison:

> In his political line in the early years he gave vent to the anger he felt. In prison he has got this anger almost totally under control. That control has come about through a deliberate effort by Mandela, for political reasons as well as personal. His warmth comes out in a real sense of concern for his comrades in prison. In an unobtrusive way he finds out if anybody has problems...Although he is completely committed to the ANC his approach to all prisoners is always warm. (International Defence and Aid Fund for Southern Africa, 1978: 194–195)

These apparent changes, however, did not suggest a loss of leadership and morale:

> His morale has been such that he has been one of the men that has inspired all who came into contact with him. He isn't the only one,

there are many who've played this role...but Nelson has been out-standing. He has had the confidence of all prisoners whatever their political persuasion and has been accepted by all of us a spokesman of the whole prisoner community...His confidence in the future has been growing. I do not recall a time when he showed any despondence or gave us any clue that he may be thinking in the back of his mind that he would never live through prison. (International Defence and Aid Fund for Southern Africa, 1978: 195)

In 1978 Mandela had already been imprisoned for a remarkable 16 years. What the accounts by Maharaj and others documented was the awe-inspiring fact that Mandela had not just endured prison in this period. On the contrary, he seemed to have "grown," politically and morally. Controlled by authorities, Mandela retained a leadership role and appeared in control of his fate. Subjected to a brutal prison regime, he stayed calm, dignified, and analytic. Faced with political criticism from fellow prisoners, he was able to see through the differences and develop personal relationships with them. Imprisoned for more than a decade and a half he remained committed, uncompromising, and convinced that the struggle would succeed. Here was a man whom the regime had tried to silence and cripple, yet by 1978 it was becoming increasingly clear that it was losing control over its prisoner and his iconic transformation. Through his exemplary life, and especially his apparent ability, developed in prison, to balance political dedication and positive personal characteristics such as caring and openness, Mandela was doing his part in providing global solidarity agents and audiences with resources for continued icon formation.

### FREEDOM AND ICONIC CLIMAX

When Mandela was finally released from prison in early 1990, he was, in a sense, a well-known stranger. As noted by Fieldhouse (2005: 122), a Gallup poll taken in 1988 revealed that no less than 92 percent of the British population knew who Mandela was (a higher percentage than those knowing their local MP). Although, as shown above, Mandela had increasingly become a global household name since the late 1970s, the man himself had played only a minor part in this process. Unable to directly address the world, information by and about Mandela had entered the public through smuggled writings, released fellow prisoners, and occasional journalistic accounts. The icon that had been created thus in a sense strongly reflected who people thought Mandela was and, perhaps not least, who they wished him to be. On his release, Mandela had, in the words of Nixon, "acquired an almost posthumous eminence" (1991: 43). But while the dead cannot do anything wrong, the living can. It was an open question whether Mandela would fit, accept, and perhaps even expand, the iconic personae created for him while serving time in prison.

The weeks and months after Mandela's release followed an almost fairytale-like plot in which the hero returns triumphant after testing and hardship. In concluding his first public speech by quoting his own final words from the Rivonia trial speech, the sense of a long formative journey coming to completion was furthered by Mandela himself. In fairytales, the hero's triumph is usually dependent on "helpers" (Campbell, 1949). At the moment of victory and/or return, these helpers must be acknowledged to highlight how the hero/icon expresses and symbolizes a certain collective idea and vision. Mandela's first speech after his release was almost entirely devoted to crediting his freedom to others and to paying homage to those who had lost their lives in the struggle: "I stand here before you not as a prophet but as a humble servant of you, the people. Your tireless and heroic sacrifices have made it possible for me to be here today. I therefore place the remaining years of my life in your hands" (quoted in *New York Times*, 1990). With formulations such as these, Mandela effectively portrayed himself as merely an instrument of a wider struggle ("I place the remaining years of my life in your hands"). While the audience may ascribe positive characteristics to the icon, he or she is expected to appear humble and unaggressive about the role (in the case of Mandela it is thus remarkable how in many speeches he uses "we" rather than "I"; see also Mandela's quote from the 1990 Wembley concert below). Any suspicion of self-aggrandizement and pursuit of personal gain (i.e., anti-collective behavior) short-circuits the iconic process. Displays of moral purity, personal sacrifice, and collective orientation are the materials that the icon must put before the audience that creates him or her. Mandela had already done so before and during his time in prison. His actions and comments as a free man powerfully underscored and expanded these qualities.

Mandela almost immediately entered the world stage that had been prepared for him. Already two months after his release, he appeared at Wembley Stadium in London for the *Nelson Mandela: An International Tribute for a Free South Africa* event and concert. On stage, Mandela was greeted like a rock star (clearly to his own surprise as he was seen giggling in disbelief during the several minutes of ovations preceding his speech). The dramatic effect of the show was transmitted to a huge transnational audience (according to Garofalo, 1992: 62, the show was broadcast in 63 countries). The concert was in a sense the popular crowning event and climax in Mandela's iconic process. It served at least two purposes. First, Mandela devoted a considerable part of his speech to eulogizing ANC president Oliver Tambo who was recovering from a stroke at the time. Following what was said above, this was intended to clearly place himself in a collective framework and, thus, to deflect attention away from his own person. Second, at several points in the speech, Mandela made it clear how the efforts of antiapartheid activists around the world had been vital to his release and the changes now sweeping across South Africa:

> Our first simple and happy task is to say thank you...Thank you that you elected not to forget, because our fate could have been a passing concern. We are here today because for almost three decades you sustained a campaign for the unconditional release of all South African political prisoners...During all the days we spent buried in the apartheid dungeons, we never lost our confidence in the certainty of our release and our victory over the apartheid system. This was because we knew that not even the hard-hearted men of Pretoria could withstand the enormous strength represented by the concerted effort of the peoples of South Africa and the rest of the world. (Mandela, 1990a)

Conjuring up an intimate and emotionally charged relationship with the crowd and the television audience, Mandela concluded his speech,

"Finally, I want to tell you...that we respect you, we admire you, and above all, we love you" (the crowd responding with extreme enthusiasm). The Wembley event thus turned out to be not only an iconic crowning of Mandela but also in a sense a self-celebration of global society and its contribution to Mandela's freedom (see Perryman, 1988: 29, for a related observation). Consider, for example, the opening remarks by American actor Denzel Washington (Washington's presence came on the back of his role as Stephen Biko in Richard Attenborough's 1987 movie about apartheid, *Cry Freedom*): "Two years ago we were here to celebrate Nelson Mandela's 70th birthday, we put our collective hearts and minds together to pray that he would be free, and today he is free" (huge roar from the crowd). The relationship between icon, agents, and audience is thus symbiotic: agents and audience create the icon but the icon is at the same time expected to call these into being, to acknowledge their contributions and to include them in a shared moral and political vision (see also the remarks in Mandela's first public speech, quoted in *New York Times*, 1990, above).

As suggested by the Denzel Washington quote, the 1990 concert was a follow-up to a concert in that same stadium only two years earlier to celebrate Mandela's seventieth birthday. Despite the fact that Mandela was still imprisoned at the time, the 1988 concert marked the beginning of the iconic climax period. It was the high point of the free-Mandela campaign that had started gaining momentum from the mid- and late 1970s, as noted above. By the late 1980s, there was a widespread conviction that the dissolution of apartheid was only a matter of time and that Mandela would soon be free to lead the final phase of the struggle. Even if Mandela was already established as a key symbol and icon in the antiapartheid struggle, there was some resistance to place Mandela on a pedestal and create what some considered a personal cult. Tony Hollingsworth, organizer of both the 1988 and 1990 events, thus had to persuade the ANC and the British Anti-Apartheid Movement (AAM) to make Mandela the symbolic center of the 1988 concert. Hollingsworth's goal was to create as big a global impact as possible (Lahusen, 1996: 100–106). This would require major broadcasters around the world to buy the show and to achieve this, Hollingsworth argued, it would be necessary to at least partly depoliticize it:

> I could understand the Anti-Apartheid Movement's position. They were very angry...They felt suspicious about it all. But I was certain that the mood of the event had to be positive. And we had to make sure that we got the broadcasters on board...My point was that a birthday-tribute, produced in a positive manner, would conform to the broadcasters' entertainment mandate and there was a good chance that they would show the full day's event. (Hollingsworth cited in Elman, n.d.)[8]

Hollingsworth hoped that inserting Mandela in the positive and celebrity-generated atmosphere of a globally broadcast birthday tribute would "sanitize" and further popularize Mandela (Hollingsworth's primary concern was that Mandela was still conceived of in the media as a "black terrorist leader"; Elman, n.d.). The show, thus, cast Mandela in universalistic terms and as a champion of human rights and democracy: absent were any references to his affiliations with communism, Marxism, and armed struggle. There is a certain element of paradox here: as noted earlier, Mandela was centrally involved in armed struggle up to his imprisonment. And in 1985, when South African president P. W. Botha offered Mandela his freedom on the condition of renouncing violence, he famously retorted by saying, "Let him renounce violence," defending people's right to use violence in situations of grave repression. Mandela and his supporters succeeded in creating a frame that on the one hand amplified the democratic and peaceful aspects and, on the other, portrayed armed struggle as justified under certain conditions. This was crucial as "violence" represents the polluted side of the peaceful-violent binary that is central to defining the scope and limits of democracy. By defending violence as a form of legitimate self-defense, Mandela and global solidarity agents were able to maintain the moral high ground and to symbolically counterpose the "good" Mandela and the "evil" apartheid regime, portraying the latter as having provoked and forced a violent response through its own violent and repressive acts (the Sharpeville massacre in 1960 in which South African police killed 69 protesters is, thus, considered a turning point in Mandela's and other activists' decision to resort to armed struggle) (see Hyslop, 2014, for an extended discussion of Mandela's view on war and violence).

As discussed above (in relation to the activities surrounding Mandela's sixtieth birthday), the 1988 concert demonstrates the importance of agency in the formation of political icons. Mandela would, of course, have been a global political icon without the 1988 and 1990 concerts. Yet there is little doubt that the Wembley events gave him a popular appeal that accelerated and amplified his iconic status. The Wembley events in turn need to be understood not as freestanding events but as culminations of popular culture's (especially in the United Kingdom and the United States) embrace of Mandela and antiapartheid since the late 1970s and early 1980s (Lahusen, 1996; Thörn, 2006: 121; Tomaselli and Boster, 1993).

The Mandela of the late 1980s and early 1990s was eminently suitable for the process of iconic climax in the new world political climate shaped by the parallel dissolution of the Cold War. Mandela was still a political activist and leader whose ultimate goal was to end the apartheid rule but he located this struggle in a clearly democratic, unideological, and conciliatory context. It should be borne in mind that when Mandela was released in 1990 it was not a given who would politically dominate South Africa in the future. Nor was it entirely clear what kind of society Mandela envisioned for the new South Africa. Thus, in early interviews, Mandela was often asked to assure that he did not strive for a one-party or Marxist state (see, e.g., Interview with the British Press, 1990). Rather, in the months following his release, Mandela made it clear that the path ahead should be paved with democracy, human rights, peace, and with black-white reconciliation:

> As we watched the staring eyes of the oppressors and the torturers, year in and year out, and felt the pain of their cruelty, year in and year out, we understood that we could not end the nightmare by surrendering ourselves to the passion of hatred and the spirit of vengeance and retribution. We understood that were we to succumb to these elemental

instincts, we would turn ourselves into a new cabal of oppressors, the instrument for the destruction of our people. We came to learn the very survival of our country demands that we proceed from a position of genuine love and respect for all our people and for all humanity. (Mandela, 1990b)

The post-release Mandela thus provided a near-perfect fit with the ascending democracy and human rights paradigm as the Cold War drew to a close. His rational and compromise seeking approach to politics not only rhymed with the time but it also resonated with fundamental Western notions of good political conduct. While a good part of Mandela's attractiveness for Western audiences was undoubtedly rooted in the extreme and exotic nature of his struggle and in a biography wildly different from most politicians and citizens in Europe and the United States, there was also something comfortably recognizable about him in his rational and moderate emphasis on democracy, human rights, dialogue, and reconciliation (Tomaselli and Boster, 1993: 3, 7). These political traits were undergirded and supported by several personal ones: first, Mandela spoke a perfect, almost old school English; second, in his many public interventions after his release he came across as an educated man able to formulate his viewpoints in elaborate and eloquent ways; and third, Mandela's public face had a warm and calm expression that seemed to parallel his political viewpoints (and to stand in contrast to his experience of repression and imprisonment).

If the 1988 and 1990 concerts were the popular crowning events in Mandela's iconic climax, the formal and official one came only three years later, in 1993, when Mandela was awarded the Nobel Peace Prize alongside Willem de Klerk. The award ceremony speech (Sejerstad, 1993) recurrently emphasized Mandela's lack of bitterness and his commitment to reconciliation, human rights, and democracy. With the peace prize, Mandela was placed in the company of others whose prizes could all be associated with the new post–Cold War emphasis on human rights and democracy (Dalai Lama in 1989, Mikhail Gorbachev in 1990, Aung San Suu Kyi in 1991, and Rigoberta Menchú in 1992). The 1988 and 1990 concerts and the Nobel Peace

Prize, the core pillars of Mandela's iconic climax, thus did not just point toward Mandela and his accomplishment but they also pointed to the world and audience that was bestowing these honors upon him. Or put differently, they expressed the political and ethical aspirations of the new world order that was emerging in the wake of the Cold War. Mandela offered a perfect vehicle for and embodiment of these ideals.

## ICONIC ESTABLISHMENT

Today, more than 20 years after the climaxing events at Wembley, Mandela maintains his status as a global political icon. With these remarks, we return to the beginning of the chapter, which noted how Mandela's death in 2013 became a genuinely global event. And when Mandela in 2010 published a book based on documents from various phases in his life, *Conversations with Myself*, it had a foreword by US president Barack Obama and drew reviews from a huge and very wide range of publications around the world. As these events indicate, Mandela apparently keeps stirring our collective and global imagination. It might in fact be argued that the sign of true iconicity is precisely the preservation of relevance and meaning outside the periods of icon formation and climax analyzed above.

There are obviously many ways to gauge global iconic establishment. A significant marker is biographical and autobiographical work. What is remarkable in the case of Mandela is how such works have in fact increased in number after the climaxing period and since he left office. For the research, a survey of Mandela-related publication was performed (this included the period 1965–2010 and English, Spanish, French, and German language publications).[9] The survey yielded 144 publications, distributed across the years in the following way: 1965 (1), 1973 (1), 1978 (2), 1980 (1), 1986 (5), 1987 (2), 1988 (2), 1989 (3), 1990 (2), 1991 (4), 1992 (3), 1993 (1), 1994 (5), 1995 (2), 1996 (3), 1997 (10), 1998 (5), 1999 (2), 2000 (5), 2001 (3), 2002 (7), 2003 (8), 2004 (6), 2005 (7), 2006 (15), 2007 (7), 2008 (8), 2009 (8), and 2010 (16). The survey indicates two things. First, the distribution of publications demonstrates that concern with and interest in Mandela at a global scale has been quite stable over a relatively long period. Second, it confirms the lead argument set out above that Mandela keeps resonating even today. While the high number of biographic publications in recent years may reflect the greater visibility of newer books in library and other databases, it is still a strong indication of Mandela's continued iconic status and establishment beyond the historical context in which it was originally forged.

Taking a closer look at these publications, a number of interesting observations emerge. Especially in the period from the late 1990s and up to the present, books appear that are part of series with titles such as Trailblazers of the Modern World; Great Lives; Days That Shook the World; Modern Heroes; Dates with History; History Makers; Front Page Lives; and People Who Made History. Titles like these both reflect and preserve Mandela's global iconicity. They convey the image of an individual who has shaped the world we live in today. Several of these publications belong in what might be termed the "pocketbook" genre. Other Mandela biographies thus appear in series such as Rookie Biographies, A Very Short Introduction To, Graphic Biographies, and Just the Fact Biographies. Importantly, these types of publications testify to the global popularization of Mandela. While in-depth knowledge must be found in the main biographies and autobiographies, the pocketbooks indicate that the global audience for Mandela is, in fact, quite broad.

What is particularly notable is Mandela's ability to survive as a global icon despite the profound changes that the world political context has undergone since the climax years. As argued earlier, Mandela's iconic climax was significantly facilitated by his fit with the post–Cold War setting and the high hopes of that time of a more peaceful world based on democracy and the respect for human rights. On a somewhat speculative note, perhaps Mandela keeps resonating precisely because he points not so much to the current time but to the past. This may at first glance seem a self-contradictory argument but it is not for the simple reason that political icons do not have fixed meanings. Today, Mandela may signify a world and a political landscape that was in many ways simpler than the present one. The struggle against apartheid was a relatively clear-cut one of good against evil and with Mandela more or less uniformly representing all that is good and just. It was never in question who had the moral high ground. Many people today may have rather vague notions about apartheid and Mandela's role in ending it, but almost one generation later, general values of justice, sacrifice, and morality remain intimately tied to his person.

## CONCLUSION

The chapter has offered a three-step analysis of formation, climax, and establishment in the iconic process of Nelson Mandela. The basic theoretical argument informing this analysis stated that icon formation occurs in interplay between the empirical background person's biography, agents, and audience. The underlying material for any iconic process is the exemplary life or biography. Yet this material needs to be developed and dramatized by political agents. For iconicity to develop on a larger scale, their work in turn must resonate with a wider audience who accepts the icon as the embodiment of certain cherished values. In the case of Mandela, the time in prison and his behavior, while incarcerated, served as a core element in his icon formation (biography). Mandela the icon, however, was largely the "product" of the global antiapartheid movement that emerged in the late 1950s and 1960s and its strategic decisions to place Mandela as the real and symbolic figurehead of the struggle against apartheid (agency). With its ability to engage popular culture, this movement was able to create wide social and political resonance for the cause of antiapartheid in general and Mandela in particular. In its climax period from approximately 1988 to 1994, the Mandela icon was strengthened and enlarged through its correspondence with globally ascendant values of democracy and human rights as the Cold War era drew to a close (audience).

The formation of Mandela, the icon, was perhaps not the primary goal of the global antiapartheid movement, but rather a by-product of specific political struggles and concerns. When antiapartheid activists staged the 1988 and 1990 Mandela concerts, they were part of a wider effort to put pressure on the apartheid regime by publicizing its injustices on a global stage. With this objective achieved, the global antiapartheid movement gradually disbanded. Yet more than 20 years later, the memory of the apartheid system and the antiapartheid struggle remains a vibrant part of the political-cultural structure of global society and one that for many is wholly or partly encapsulated in the figure of Nelson Mandela. Mandela the icon is a complex landscape with multiple connection points between the three theoretical elements outlined in the chapter: biography, agency, and audience. While its basic element is the exemplary empirical life of the man Mandela, the icon not only points to and emphasizes these elements but it also points to its creators. This two-way street is crucial to appreciate the argument about the relationship between icons and global society. Mandela the icon, in other words, represents the lived values and qualities of the man, yet it also represents who "we" as a global community wish to be. In that sense, as discussed in the "Freedom and Iconic Climax" subsection, the freeing of Mandela was (and is) to at least some extent seen as the result of the efforts of a global society working in unison. Global society, expressed in social movement action, created the icon and now it not only serves as an emblem commemorating Mandela and the wider struggle against apartheid but also the power of global society and its ability to protect and expand cherished political values.

Finally, it is worth highlighting three issues that were not directly addressed in the chapter but have relevance for the book's broader discussion of global society (they are further discussed in the book's concluding chapter). First, it is notable how Mandela on closer scrutiny is part of a symbolic family (see chapter 1) that includes a number of politically symbolized places (e.g., Robben Island), events (e.g., the Sharpeville massacre), and photographs (e.g., the photographs of Hector Pieterson; see chapter 1). An extended analysis of Mandela as a global political icon could usefully explore the interconnections to these other symbols and the way they infuse each other with meaning. Second, it is vital to remember that while Mandela is clearly a global icon, such an analytical focus should not be seen as an attempt to denationalize Mandela, as it were. As shown especially in the "Prison and Icon Formation" subsection, Mandela was a national symbol and icon before he became a global one. Third, the chapter has adopted a rather uncritical approach to Mandela's icon formation. There are several reasons and possibilities for engaging critically with the insights presented in the chapter. It was noted above how Mandela the icon is a creation of global society and a global social movement. This clearly begs the question of who actually constitutes global society. It is thus evident that the global antiapartheid movement was primarily based in Europe and the United States. This observation suggests that so-called global political icons often have a certain geographic bias and, most importantly, that they potentially are forged in a process of meaning adaptation in which the icon is shaped in the image of its creators (this theme is more thoroughly addressed in chapter 5). In line with this observation, it is pertinent to consider how iconic processes per definition entail some degree of idolization. While idolization is not necessarily problematic per se, it does potentially entail a focus deflection from the collective and structural to the individual and particular. Elevating Mandela in the way analyzed in this chapter has many sound reasons, but it may also generate a perception that the end of apartheid was more or less the result of one man's efforts, when it was in fact brought about through the collective effort by South Africans, many of whom paid with their lives without receiving the same iconic status as Mandela (this theme is revisited in the concluding chapter 6).

# CHAPTER 3

# GRIEVANCE COMMUNITIES

SINCE ITS INCEPTION AT THE BEGINNING OF THE SO-CALLED WAR on terror in 2002, the detention camp at Guantanamo Bay has been subjected to harsh criticism and condemnation from many quarters. Guantanamo Bay has had a decidedly global status from the outset because of its central role in the post–9/11 war on terror. This site of perceived injustice is populated with prisoners of multiple nationalities, who were forcefully moved there from battlefields and localities all over the world. Guantanamo Bay was thus born with significant potential as a global injustice symbol (as such it fits the *circumvention pattern* described in chapter 1 but with a twist in the sense that Guantanamo is an "implant" whose perceived injustices are not directly linked to or in its geographic location). For actors within political Islam, it symbolizes the unjust nature of Western policies, historically as well as contemporarily, toward Muslims and the Muslim world. For jihadist terrorist organizations (which are considered here as a form of *activist* organizations) like, for example, al-Qaeda, Guantanamo Bay is repeatedly invoked as a mobilizing injustice symbol, legitimating and inspiring terrorist action (Corman, 2009, thus reports 26 al-Qaeda communications from 2002 to 2008 making direct references to the Guantanamo Bay detention center). Even terrorists, the most indiscriminate and ruthless form of activism, thus devote considerable energy to legitimate their actions to a wider public and to locate their claims in existing and well-known political-cultural schemas. As such they engage in what was referred to in chapter 1 as *moral-political action*. The term "moral" may seem controversial in relation to an organization whose political strategy involves the killing of random and innocent people. Yet, as argued in chapter 1, moral does not mean good in a specific sense. It rather suggests that action is motivated by shared conceptions of what is right and wrong, good and bad. The definition and content of these categories, as is well known, vary historically as well as between organizations and collectives.

Jihadist terrorists, and especially, al-Qaeda, have since the 1990s established themselves as genuinely global actors catering to globally dispersed audiences (Gerges, 2005; Juergensmeyer, 2005; Roy, 2004; Sageman, 2004, 2008; Tuman, 2010).[1] Global injustice symbols, it is argued, have been and continue to be central in this process. This potential has not been lost on policy makers either. In a September 2010 speech on his (still unfulfilled) ambition to close the Guantanamo Bay detention center, US president Barack Obama underlined its role in jihadist terrorism:

> One of the most powerful tools we have to keep the American people safe is not providing al-Qaeda and jihadists recruiting tools...And Guantanamo is probably the number one recruitment tool that is used by these jihadist organizations. And we see it in the websites that they put up. We see it in the messages that they're delivering. (Obama, 2010)[2]

While Guantanamo Bay (and other global injustice symbols such as Abu Ghraib and the Muhammad cartoons) can thus be argued to provide immediate symbolic and ideational support for jihadist action, the chapter seeks to couch this point in a wider sociological framework. It argues and demonstrates how injustice symbols such as Guantanamo Bay are core elements in a political Islamist *grievance community* with global extension. Grievance communities, initially defined, are physical and/or virtual networks of people and organizations ideationally connected through shared injustice perceptions and identities. This can obviously be studied in various ways. The chapter's guiding argument is that injustice symbols are central in constituting the *meaning infrastructure* of grievance communities. The political Islamist grievance community cannot, as discussed further below, be reduced to jihadist terrorism. Yet it is contended that jihadist terrorists are anchored in this grievance community and the political-cultural schemas that provide its ideational foundation. This relationship is *dialectical* (see chapter 1). Jihadist terrorism thus draws strongly on already existing and historically rooted political-cultural schemas, but given its influence it also recreates and expands them. It is often claimed that the post–9/11 situation has been one of global jihad. This concept is typically rooted in observations of the globally networked character of contemporary jihadist terrorism (e.g., Sageman, 2004, 2008). The chapter does not refute or criticize this perspective, but by coupling it with the concepts of injustice symbols and grievance communities, it offers a distinctly sociological and political-cultural answer to what is global about global jihad. While the chapter focuses empirically on al-Qaeda, this organization is seen as part of a wider *global social movement* motivated by the critique and condemnation of Guantanamo Bay.

The ambition of the chapter is thus interrelatedly twofold: first, it analyzes a number of key elements in the way Guantanamo Bay has been constructed by al-Qaeda as a major global injustice symbol; second, it builds on these observations to discuss Guantanamo Bay's location in a global grievance community based in political Islam (this discussion is primarily taken up in the conclusion). The chapter begins with a conceptual and theoretical elaboration of the term "grievance community" and its relationship with that of injustice symbols. It then discusses political Islam as a grievance community. Moving on to the case study of Guantanamo Bay, it focuses on four analytical elements: (a) the creation of moral-political categories and binaries in relation to Guantanamo Bay; (b) its location in a wider injustice hierarchy; (c) the role of visuality; and (d) the invocation of solidarity within political Islam. The analysis focuses on the discursive activities of al-Qaeda. It concludes with a discussion of political Islam and Guantanamo Bay in relation to the concept of global society. In it the empirical field is opened up to highlight the contestation and conflict surrounding Guantanamo Bay at a global level.

## GLOBAL GRIEVANCE COMMUNITIES

The theoretical and conceptual section consists of two parts. The first outlines the concept of grievance communities and its relation with the concept of injustice symbols. This is done at a general level. The second relates it to the political-cultural schema of political Islam.

### GRIEVANCE COMMUNITIES AND INJUSTICE SYMBOLS

Grievance communities are communities that (a) have generated social and political belief and meaning systems that fundamentally challenge what they consider to be dominant authority systems; (b) are "united," physically and/or virtually, primarily through shared perceptions of injustice and injustice-oriented political-cultural schemas; (c) display a strong identity element; and (d) are not predominantly organized or represented through political parties, interest organizations, and social movements. Continuing from point (d), the concept of grievance communities is useful precisely because it allows us to capture and analyze political phenomena that cannot be fully comprehended through the actor and organizationally oriented conceptual vocabulary of parties, interest organizations, and social movements. It is akin as such to Fraser's (1992, 1995) concept of subaltern counterpublics. Fraser developed the idea of alternative public spheres as a critique of Habermas's (1962) notion of a bourgeois public sphere dominated by middle- and upper-class males. Fraser thus argued that parallel with the bourgeois public sphere in, especially, the nineteenth century, there existed alternative public spheres created by and made up of groups and individuals marginalized in and/or excluded from public life and the political process: in particular, workers and women. Of course, both workers and women are now fully integrated in the political process. Yet in the early phase of their political mobilization and before the building and acquirement of more formalized and organized representation, these groups constituted grievance communities centered around and forged through alternative public spheres. Today, while we do not have any strict parallels with these historical experiences, it makes sense to think of, for example, the extreme-right- and left-wing autonomous movements, and, as discussed in more detail later, political Islam as grievance communities and alternative public spheres. Speaking of these phenomena as grievance *communities* does not mean that they are *organizationally* amorphous. On the contrary, their infrastructure is generally created and maintained by various groups, organizations, and other types of actors that professionally or semiprofessionally promote the ideas of the community and which may in certain situations act together and take on social movement forms (further elaboration follows). Yet, as suggested in point (d) above, it is a defining aspect of grievance communities that they are also constituted by individuals not necessarily involved in organized activities, but directly or indirectly associated through their adherence to certain political-cultural schemas and injustice perceptions (as expressed, e.g., in politically oriented lifestyles).

Grievance communities can be both physical and virtual (in reality these aspects typically combine). From a global perspective, the latter is of particular interest. On the one hand, interaction among individuals and organizations is mediated through various forms of communication technology, including both old and new media. On the other, and in a wider sociological sense, individuals and organizations see themselves as part of an imagined community (Anderson, 1983) of likeminded individuals and organizations. A *global* grievance community is thus characterized by injustice perceptions and identities that cut across national and regional divides. Imagined and global grievance communities such as these require shared *injustice symbols* to provide internal coherence and visibility in their meaning systems. Given the largely imagined nature of global grievance communities, it might plausibly be argued that there is a particularly pronounced need for symbols that can serve as common reference and orientation points. Injustice symbols associated with grievance communities generally have an affirmative nature. They are symbols that represent and confirm the community's interpretation of injustice. Therefore, they often play a role as *mobilizing symbols* for the movement-oriented elements of the grievance community. They are employed, in other words, to support not only claims about injustice but also call for action (recall, e.g., Barack Obama's quote about Guantanamo mentioned above). As a result, such injustice symbols are generally fiercely contested and subjected to de-symbolization activities by the authority system that the community defines itself in negative relation to.

## THE POLITICAL-CULTURAL SCHEMA OF POLITICAL ISLAM

The term "political Islam" is both controversial and complex. Controversial, because by locating jihadist organizations within it, as discussed above, a link is inadvertently made between violence and the religion of Islam. It is therefore crucial at the outset to underline that the chapter does not propose any kind of automatic or natural connection between Islam and political violence. The term "political Islam" includes but is much broader than "terrorist jihadism." It is defined here as an ideological worldview in which religious ideas dominate and guide political ideas and action. Evidently, political Islam is not one single movement or unified ideology. Under the rubric, we thus find several political actors and political theories that differ significantly in terms of both goals and methods (Ayoob, 2008; Wickham, 2005). The concept of grievance community offers a theoretical and conceptual compromise between those who claim that overarching terms are inherently reductive and politically problematic (Crone, Gad, and Sheikh, 2008) and those who argue that political Islam is a more or less coherent and singular historical phenomenon and movement (e.g., Mozaffari, 2007). A political Islam–based grievance community may thus be defined as those individuals and collectives that subscribe to the above understanding of the relationship between religion and politics *and* see this vision as being unjustly opposed by a system of authority. Belonging to such a grievance community, as underlined in the preceding section, does not presuppose active political participation. Nor does it, to reiterate the above cautionary remark, imply employment or acceptance of violent political means.

To be able to speak of political Islam as a grievance community, we need to identify a shared *political-cultural schema* (see chapter 1). Given the diversity of the grievance community, identifying such a schema is necessarily an exercise in complexity reduction. Nevertheless, it is possible to highlight a number of themes more or less shared across the community and flowing from the definition of political Islam offered above. The overarching political-cultural schema of political Islam is negatively defined vis-à-vis Western (primarily symbolized by the United States) modernity (Juergensmeyer, 2005). It is thus opposed to or skeptical of the following: (a) the separation between state and religion, including the prominence of political ideas over religious ones; (b) equality between the sexes; and (c) capitalist consumerism. These elements are all hallmarks of the Western modern social and political experience. In the political-cultural schema of political Islam these three elements are integrated with two additional ones: (d) the claim that these social and political values have been and are being forced on the Muslim world, either through political and military power or through the globalization of Western consumer culture and patterns; and (e) the desire for a new social and political (world) order in which Islamic ideas form and dominate society's value and legal structure. According to Ayoob (2008) such visions are often rooted in a political reimagination of a past golden age.

   It is point (d) in particular that makes it relevant to speak of a *grievance* community. Recalling the preceding section, grievance communities are thus premised on their relationship with a system of authority that violates core values of the community. Within the political-cultural schema of political Islam, this system of authority is, broadly speaking, the West—that is, primarily Europe and the United States. Contemporarily as well as historically, the relationship between the West and the Muslim world is viewed as characterized by unjust aggression, expansion, and dominance. Historically, this understanding has deep roots in the Crusades of the eleventh to thirteenth centuries. In the contemporary situation it is particularly founded, as discussed later, in the war against terrorism since 9/11 and, especially, the military presence in Iraq and Afghanistan. The West's influence not only radiates from the geographic West but it is also encountered in the Muslim world itself where several states (such as Egypt under Hosni Mubarak and Saudi Arabia) were/are seen as overly influenced by or even puppets of the West (Juergensmeyer, 2005). This understanding was popularized and politically amplified with Ayatollah Khomeini's toppling of the United States backed Shah Reza Pahlavi in Iran in 1979 (see also chapter 5). The schema rests on a number of moral-political *binaries* (see chapters 1 and 2) that serve to portray the authority system (and its vassals) as morally and politically corrupt and unjust: clean-unclean, true-false, honest-dishonest, victim-aggressor, Muslims-infidels, and believers-nonbelievers (see also Alexander, 2004d). Sketching such an overarching schema, as already suggested, does not imply internal coherence or unity in analysis and action within the schema. The same schema can and does support a broad range of interpretations and political methods. The grievance community concept is useful here because it allows us to capture how political Islam is highly internally diverse, yet builds on a number of tenets that are widely shared, temporally and geographically.

The grievance community of political Islam is genuinely global. It is so in at least two ways. First, several authors (e.g., Roy, 2004) have noted how political Islam is deterritorialized in the sense that its members are globally dispersed and in many cases live outside the Muslim world, including in the West where many countries have a high proportion of Muslim citizens and migrants. Second, the solutions offered within political Islam are generally not about a retreat to the local or the national but build on regional and global political visions modeled, as noted earlier, on the past. The grievance community of political Islam is thus strongly anchored in the notion of the Umma. The Umma is a concept with varying meanings (and originally does not have political connotation), but at the most basic level it refers to a global, largely imagined, community of Muslims that, in a sense, overrules national, social, and political differences (Mandaville, 2003). Many activists within political Islam thus envision the installment of a new Caliphate uniting Muslims, culturally as well as politically, across the globe (Ayoob, 2008) (although it should be noted that these visions are often and conflictually defined along the division between Sunni and Shia interpretations of Islam). The global grievance community is at least partly constituted and nurtured through the media, especially new media developments such as global television channels catering mainly to a Muslim audience and the emergence of Internet-based communication platforms (Shavit, 2009: ch. 6). The point, of course, is not that the media have created the global grievance community of political Islam. This community, as shown above, has deep historical roots, but there is little doubt that opportunities for cross-border communication and visibility have expanded the community's potential global range.

As noted earlier, grievance communities are not actors in themselves. Nevertheless, they do have a significant action component in that they consist of and are defined by various organized political actors. The range of actors associated with political Islam and who subscribe, in broad terms, to the political-cultural schema outlined above is diverse and includes states, activists, political parties, media organizations, and networked citizens (see chapter 1). Sometimes these actors act more or less independently. In other cases they converge, briefly or more permanently, around certain issues to form what according to the definition outlined in chapter 1 may be seen as (global) social movements. Guantanamo Bay–related action is an example of a more permanent type of social movement mobilization. The former, brief, type occurred, for example, in relation to the Danish Muhammad cartoons in early 2006. While the empirical focus of this chapter is on Guantanamo Bay, we may identify several other, admittedly very different, injustice symbols broadly anchored in the political-cultural schema of political Islam: Palestine, Abu Ghraib (see chapter 1), Mohamed al-Durrah (see chapter 1), *The Satanic Verses*, and, recently, the Danish Muhammad cartoons, to mention just a few examples.[3]

## AL-QAEDA AND GUANTANAMO BAY

This section is divided into seven subsections: the first offers a brief methodological note; the second describes the historical background of the Guantanamo Bay detention camp; the third discusses jihadist terrorism as a form of activism and its relation to social movements; the fourth shows how al-Qaeda mobilizes Guantanamo to expose the *moral corruption* of their opponents; the fifth locates Guantanamo in a wider *injustice hierarchy*; the sixth argues how Guantanamo is part of a *family* of event- and place-based injustice symbols that draw on the *power of visualization*; and the seventh subsection concludes on these observations through the theoretical prism of *global grievance communities*.

Methodologically, the analysis that follows primarily builds on written and verbal statements by leading figures in al-Qaeda: primarily Osama bin Laden (killed by US special forces in 2011), Ayman al-Zawahiri (leader of al-Qaeda since the death of bin Laden), and Abu al-Libi (killed in a US drone strike in 2012). This material has been collected in two ways. First, a number of al-Qaeda's public interventions can be found in a series of volumes published by the IntelCenter.[4] Some of these are available electronically, allowing for keyword searches and so on. Second, the Internet provides a number of empirical materials. Since many al-Qaeda communiqués are not issued in writing but through voice recordings and video, jihadist websites as well as YouTube were key sources in the collection of data. The goal of this analysis has not been to trace the development of the Guantanamo injustice symbol since its inception in 2002. As a result, the empirical material subjected to analysis does not have a temporal or sequential logic. Rather, focus has been on uncovering moral-political patterns in the way al-Qaeda discursively employs and creates the Guantanamo injustice symbol.

## BACKGROUND

Guantanamo Bay is geographically part of Cuba but has been leased by the United States since 1903. The lease agreement followed the Spanish-American war and was confirmed in a 1934 treaty. The treaty allows the United States to use the area for coaling or naval stations as long as required, in practice making the lease indefinite. Guantanamo Bay is a naval base but was used in the 1990s as a detention camp for Haitian and Cuban refugees and asylum seekers (Gregory, 2006: 411–412; Johns, 2005: 616). In January 2002, shortly after the beginning of the war in Afghanistan, the United States started transferring persons captured on the battlefield to Guantanamo. The base was used by the Bush administration because it was initially considered to be outside of the US legal jurisdiction. In 2006 in the court case *Hamdan* (a detainee at Guantanamo Bay) *v. Rumsfeld*, the US Supreme Court ruled that this assertion did not conform to the Uniform Code of Military Justice and the Geneva Convention. Guantanamo is part of a global pattern of CIA-run so-called black sites. Black sites are facilities outside the United States where detainees from the war on terror are being held and interrogated for intelligence purposes. These sites remain shrouded in secrecy but it is widely believed that such sites have been in operation in several countries around the world, including in Europe (for an account of the early phase of the detention camp, see Greenberg, 2009; for a wider historical perspective, see Carvin, 2010; for a collection of papers and statements by detainees, see Worthington, 2007). US president Barack Obama entered the presidency on promises to gradually close Guantanamo. This process set in motion in early 2009 has been severely restricted, partly due to resistance from parts of the US Congress. In total, 779 detainees have been held at Guantanamo, with a peak of 700 (Bowker and Kaye, 2007). This number has gradually declined as detainees have been released and acquitted. Only 7 detainees have been formally convicted; and of the remaining detainees only 6 face formal charges (Human Rights Watch, 2013a). In the final report for the Guantanamo Review Task Force (2010), 48 detainees were designated for indefinite detainment because they were considered too dangerous to be released. At the time of writing (June 2013), 166 detainees remain at Guantanamo. Of these, 86 (mainly Yemenis) have already been cleared for release. In the spring of 2013, 103 detainees went on a hunger strike to protest conditions and the delay in proceedings and releases. The hunger strike pushed Barack Obama to reopen the debate and proceedings to have the detention facility closed down and to speed up release procedures for those cleared.

## JIHADIST TERRORISM AND ACTIVISM

Jihadist terrorism is not a new phenomenon. Yet it has acquired unprecedented centrality at a global scale since al-Qaeda's 9/11 attacks. The sense of threat generated by this momentous attack has been maintained by other, if comparably less serious, al-Qaeda attacks in Western countries (in particular the 2004 Madrid and 2005 London attacks on public transportation). While it may seem controversial, jihadist terrorists (and terrorists in general) are activists, albeit in a qualified way. Tarrow (1998: 3) probably did not have terrorists in mind when he defined activism as a strategy "used by people who lack regular access to institutions, who act in the name of new or unaccepted claims, and who behave in ways that fundamentally challenge others or authorities." Yet, unless we want to employ a normative yardstick to the category of activism, terrorists fit this description just as well as the usual good suspects of activism research: for example, environmentalists, women, human rights activists, and so on.[5] Of course, caution should be taken to not exaggerate the similarities. Terrorist activism most notably stands out from most other forms of activism in its redemptive use of activists' lives (suicide terrorism) and its random killing of civilians. Despite their extreme and fundamentally antidemocratic nature, terrorists, like most other forms of activism, do engage in public communication activities aimed at legitimating goals and strategies. Jihadist terrorists operate on at least two communicative levels. First, the terrorist act is a form of symbolic communication in its own right (e.g., Alexander, 2004d; Juergensmeyer, 2000: ch. 7; Schmid and de Graaf, 1982; Tuman, 2010). Second, even if the terrorist event is not always immediately tied to written or verbal statements, jihadist terrorist organizations, as mentioned, do engage in public discursive contests (e.g., Snow and Byrd, 2007). Jihadist political communication has two interrelated dimensions: to explain/legitimize their acts to a wider public and to recruit and inspire new activists. These legitimation and mobilizing activities and their construction and employment of the Guantanamo Bay injustice symbol are at the center of the discussions that follow. While al-Qaeda thus fulfills the criteria for being considered an activist organization, it should also, according to the definition set out in chapter 1, and following what was said on political Islam in the "Political-Cultural Schema of Political Islam" subsection, be seen as part of a wider global social movement around Guantanamo Bay. This movement cannot be reduced to any single organization or actor but includes all of the categories outlined in chapter 1 (activist organizations, media, parties, states, international institutions, and networked citizens).[6]

MORAL CORRUPTION

As discussed in chapter 1 and the theoretical sections, injustice symbols have a decidedly moral-political character. In the political-cultural schema of political Islam, this is reflected in a set of binaries
that cast the West, and especially the United States, as *morally corrupt*. This discursive pattern is a staple in al-Qaeda's employment of
Guantanamo Bay, which serves to expose the purported hypocrisy
of the West. In a video aired on Al-Jazeera on February 20, 2005,
Ayman al-Zawahiri (2008a: 118) thus contended that Guantanamo
"reveals the reality of reform and democracy which America claims
that it seeks to spread in our countries. This reform will be based
on US detention centers—like Bagram, Kandahar, Guantanamo and
Abu-Ghuryab."[7] What is laid bare, in other words, is a perceived gap
between the (false) democratic intentions of the West and their actual
behavior: "What is occurring at Guantanamo Bay is a historic scandal
for America and its values, as the shouts ring in your ears: You hypocrites, what is the point of your signing of any treaty or your abiding
by any accord?" (al-Zawahiri, 2008b: 77). This letter (titled "Letter to
the Americans: Why Do We Fight and Resist You?") from al-Zawahiri, and read by Adam Gadahn on video on January 7, 2006, portrays
the United States as morally suspicious (they violate their own values)
and in disregard of international law. The preceding quote is thus
followed up by the following statement: "You are a nation without
values, principles, or morals, and...these things, as you understand
them, are what you expect of others and not what you yourselves must
abide by." However, it is not only the United States that is implicated
in the moral and legal morass but the UN too "is silent in total col-
lusion with what is happening in Abu Ghrayb, Guantanamo, and
Bagram and the treatment meted out to the al-Qaida and Taliban
prisoners...Where are the international accords and charters and the
rights of man?" (al-Zawahiri, 2008c: 25; video interview on as-Sahab,
September 19, 2005).[8] The recurring reference to national and international laws and values in these discursive activities does not imply
adherence to or acceptance of them. They are included to expose the
hypocrisy and double-tongued nature of al-Qaeda's opponents: "Bush

called on us to respect human rights while he is establishing secret prisons everywhere, exercising dirty torture in Bagram, Abu Ghraib, and Guantanamo" (al-Zawahiri, 2008d: 90; video statement originally from 2006). Guantanamo Bay maintains a prominent role in al-Qaeda's communications and has acquired renewed relevance in the context of the hunger strike in 2013 (see the "Background" subsection above). In a video circulated on jihadist websites in the summer of 2013, al-Zawahiri claimed, "The (hunger) strike by our brothers at Guantanamo unmasks the true ugly face of (the United States of) America" (cited in Reuters, 2013). Al-Qaeda clearly thinks in terms of global audiences as it criticizes Guantanamo. In a video interview aired as early as October 2002, al-Zawahiri thus claims, "The whole world is witness to the Guantanamo Bay masquerade and the comedy of hundreds detained without any charge or court hearing in America" (al-Zawahiri, 2008e: 12). And in a later audio statement from 2004, Osama bin Laden echoes this view by pointing out how Guantanamo has "moved the whole of mankind" (bin Laden, 2008: 84).

Guantanamo Bay is thus constructed as an *injustice* symbol by discursively associating it with the immoral behavior ("historic *scandal*," "you *hypocrites*," "*dirty* torture," "*ugly* face") of, especially, the United States. The immorality claim is based on the United States' apparent disregard for its own stated values as well as its trampling on core Muslim values, such as the 2005 events when a number of instances of Quran desecration at Guantanamo were reported and later confirmed: "This ignorance, which causes the people of the West to…voice their approval when their armies desecrate copies of the Koran in Guantanamo, and their yellow press and televangelists insult our Prophet Muhammad, peace be upon Him" (Azzam al Amriki, 2006 quoted in Corman, 2009). This moral and value-oriented line of argumentation is not only dominant in Guantanamo-related statements but is also a general and recurring feature in al-Qaeda's communication. Recalling the argument that the Guantanamo symbol is anchored in the political-cultural schema of political Islam, it is notable when glancing at the above quotes that they do not explicitly invoke religiously based claims (except perhaps from that pointing to the desecration of the Quran). Yet they draw strongly on point

(d) discussed in the "Political-Cultural Schema of Political Islam" sub-section, which concerns the conviction that the West and the United States in particular, are pursuing an aggressive, unjust, and immoral global strategy of subjugating Muslims. Guantanamo is presented and constructed as a core symbol of this strategy, which disregards the West's own values (as well as those of all Muslims) and is premised on the universally disdained mismatch between words and action.

INJUSTICE HIERARCHIES

In chapter 1, it was argued how injustice symbols are often related in "families." Extending on this we may consider Guantanamo Bay to be part of a wider *injustice hierarchy*. Guantanamo Bay and other prison facilities repeatedly mentioned by al-Qaeda, mainly Abu Ghraib and Bagram, are specific places and events. Yet, as suggested by the quotes above, the injustices committed there are highlighted by al-Qaeda to *condense* a much wider situation of injustice. There are at least two levels to be noted here. At the first level, Guantanamo and the other detention centers condense the unjust nature of the wars and occupations in Afghanistan and Iraq and of the so-called global war on terror in general. To the outside observer and potential al-Qaeda activist/terrorist/sympathizer, wars and occupations are relatively abstract, especially when, as is the case with these recent wars and occupations, there is no clearly identifiable front line and hostilities have a low-intensity character (minor clashes and attacks, but rarely large-scale and protracted battles). References to concrete and visible places and prisons such as Guantanamo Bay, Abu Ghraib, and Bagram are symbolic and cognitive shortcuts to identify what is problematic about the Afghanistan and Iraq wars and occupations: the West's military and political violation of Muslim countries, populations, and values ("the reality of reform and democracy which America claims that it seeks to spread in our countries"; see al-Zawahiri, 2008a: 118, quote above). At the second (and widest) level, Western military/political presences in Afghanistan and Iraq are employed by al-Qaeda, often through the invocation of Guantanamo Bay, Abu Ghraib, and Bagram, as symbols of a historically continuous attempt by the West to subjugate

Muslims and Islamic culture (the historical dimension is particularly evident in al-Qaeda's use of Palestine as an injustice symbol and in the repeated labeling of the United States and its allies as "crusaders" and "crusader nations"). Condensation, in this sense, is *universalization* (see chapter 1). Guantanamo Bay, for example, represents an injustice in itself, but through contextualization it is simultaneously presented as a symptom of a much broader and historically anchored problematic. In sum, Guantanamo and the other detention centers may be considered part of an injustice hierarchy with Guantanamo Bay, Abu Ghraib, and Bagram constituting the micro-level; Afghanistan and Iraq, the meso-level; and the historical conflict between Islam and the West, the macro-level.

Guantanamo Bay, consequently, does not enjoy privileged injustice symbolic status for al-Qaeda. As argued above, al-Qaeda employs many different symbols, and often in combination (some of the most popular were mentioned in the "Political-Cultural Schema of Political Islam" subsection). Consider, for example, this statement by al-Zawahiri (quoted in BBC, 2006) following the death of protesters in Kabul:

> My Muslim brothers in Kabul, the latest US aggression against you was preceded by a long series of the killing of innocent people in Kabul, Khost, Uruzgan, Helmand, Kandahar, and Konar. This aggression was also preceded by torturing Muslims in Kandahar and Bagram and at the prison of darkness in Kabul. This was also preceded by insulting the holy Koran in Bagram and Guantanamo and by the Danish, French, and Italian mocking of the noblest prophet, God's peace and blessings be upon him.

The master injustice symbol in al-Qaeda's discursive activities (and those of most other jihadist organizations) is probably Palestine. It occurs in one way or the other in most of al-Qaeda's public interventions. Palestine's prominent location in the symbolic vocabulary of political Islam owes to its highly visible status at the global scene and to its deeper symbolic roots that go all the way to the Crusades. The juxtaposition of symbols in al-Qaeda's discursive activities demonstrates the point outlined in chapter 1 that symbols morally and politically enforce each other. This juxtaposition thus has a clearly strategic purpose in which audience resonance is enhanced by association with firmly grounded symbols, yet it cannot be reduced to purely instrumental thinking: an injustice symbol such as Palestine is a defining and internalized element in the schema of political Islam and, consequently, a foundational part of the political identity of those subscribing to it.

IMAGES

As demonstrated by several of the above quotes Guantanamo is often mentioned alongside other detention facilities, especially Abu Ghraib and Bagram.[9] In this, al-Qaeda draws strongly on the potential for moral-political resonance created by the Abu Ghraib scandal— another powerful injustice symbol in the claims making and legitimation efforts of al-Qaeda and other jihadist groups (as such the argument here on symbolic families continues that of the preceding subsection). Abu Ghraib, now formally known as Baghdad Central Prison, is located in Iraq. It became known to a wider public in 2004 when American media (CBS and *The New Yorker*) reported on and photographically documented widespread prisoner abuse at the facility (Laustsen, 2006). The Abu Ghraib photographs have attained global symbolic and iconic status. They are part of a pantheon of commemorative images that shape people's memories and opinions about the war on terror post–9/11. Although the same degree of extralegal abuse has not been documented (or at least not photographically documented) for Guantanamo, their juxtaposition and indirect comparison has an evident associative and culturally resonant effect. Much of this effect draws on the power of visualization. Again, even if the images that emerged from Abu Ghraib are arguably more extreme than those related to Guantanamo, the latter has its own well-known imagery of cage-like outdoor cells and orange-clad shackled prisoners. The visual aspect serves two potential roles in al-Qaeda's mobilization of the Guantanamo injustice symbol. First, the worldwide diffusion of Guantanamo-related images allows al-Qaeda messages and claims to tap into and activate existing visual knowledge of primarily Guantanamo, but also, as suggested above, in an indirect sense, Abu Ghraib: "And the pictures of our captives in Abu Ghurayb, Guantanamo and Bagram continue to be present in the mind of every Muslim in whose limbs the spirit of faith creeps" (al-Libi, 2007; audio message). Second, the images themselves may be, and are, used actively in video/image-based or supported messages. The 2013 hunger strike at Guantanamo Bay has generated its own visual vocabulary. This is primarily related to the force-feeding procedures installed by US authorities. While few images of the force-feeding itself are available, several images of the instruments used in the procedure have been circulated globally, including that of a restraint chair resembling an electric chair. Most of the images coming out of Guantanamo Bay point to the unjust exercise of power by an authority system, which, as noted in chapter 1, is at the root of all injustice symbols. Images of prison cells, barbed wire, surveillance towers, the anonymity of prison uniforms, instruments for force feeding are the images of power and authority at work. While such images are not *in flagranti* (see chapter 1) images showing unjust authority in action (in contrast to those from Abu Ghraib), their neutrality is nevertheless partly suspended and politicized in the context of discursive arguments pointing to the illegal and illegitimate nature of Guantanamo Bay. The discursive and visual dimensions thus mutually reinforce each other in the overall moral-political argumentation pattern (it should be noted that the visual dimension is utilized not only by al-Qaeda and other actors within political Islam but also by actors working on the basis of other political-cultural schemas; see the conclusion).

GRIEVANCE COMMUNITIES AND SOLIDARITY

"The Political-Cultural Schema of Political Islam" subsection pointed out how, within Islam, a conception of a common global identity already exists: the Umma. Al-Qaeda recurrently invokes this universal category. How to define the Umma is, as noted, a point of some controversy among Muslims and Muslim clerics and scholars (Mandaville, 2003). For example, it becomes clear when analyzing al-Qaeda's use of the concept that this organization employs it in a highly politicized manner. While their communications are directed to broad audiences (e.g., "Muslim brothers everywhere"), partaking in al-Qaeda's understanding of the Umma seems predicated upon one's willingness to engage in global jihad, that is, to take up arms and mobilize against injustice: "And I tell the Muslim Umma: if we don't resist, we shall be finished. Resistance is a must, and this resistance can be nothing but a popular one at the hands of the Muslim Umma, because the governments are treasonous" (al-Zawahiri, 2008f: 188; video statement originally from December 2006). As suggested by the quote, and as mentioned in the "Political-Cultural Schema of Political Islam" subsection, the responsibility to the Umma transcends national boundaries and state allegiances. For al-Qaeda the large majority of states in the Muslim world are traitors to Islam and puppets of the West (192). The only true social and political-religious unit, in other words, is the Umma.

Even if the term is not explicitly used by al-Qaeda, these claims build on a global conception of *solidarity*. Khosrokhavar (2005: 153) gestures importantly in this direction when he speaks about contemporary jihadists as motivated by a "humiliation by proxy": feelings of indignation and moral shocks arising from witnessing injustices committed against distant others with whom one iden-tifies. This process is actively nurtured by al-Qaeda leaders who recurrently point to the injustices committed against Muslims in Guantanamo, Palestine, Iraq, Afghanistan, Chechnya, and countless other places, and how responding to this suffering and injustice is the duty of all true Muslims. The active expression of this duty is jihad. In a 2007 video statement on contemporary jihad in Iraq, Abu Yahya al-Libi (2009: 46) underlines how this struggle cannot be confined to Iraq: "Beloved Mujahid brothers, your blessed Jihad...isn't the Jihad of the Iraqi people alone...it is the Jihad of the entire Islamic Umma." As argued earlier, all jihadist struggles are interlinked in al-Qaeda's interpretation. For example, al-Libi continues, jihad in Iraq is also "the Jihad of the confined captive who has swallowed lump after lump of humiliation, insult, suppression and severity at the hands of the worshippers of the Cross and their hirelings in Abu Ghrayb, Guantanamo, Bagram." These observations underline why it is relevant to speak about al-Qaeda's understanding of the Umma as a global grievance community. It is a global community united primarily through a shared sense of injustice and a solidaristic commitment to those who suffer under these injustices. These latter points set the scene for and are expanded upon in the conclusion, which takes up some of the broader implications, theoretically and empirically, of what has been analyzed until now.

## CONCLUSION

The chapter has argued that the Guantanamo Bay detention center is a core injustice symbol in the discursive activities of al-Qaeda (and other actors based in the political-cultural schema of political Islam). It was demonstrated that the symbol is (a) constructed via a range of moral-political binaries exposing the moral corruption of the West; (b) located at the micro-level of a wider injustice hierarchy in which Guantanamo is seen as a symbol of the injustices related to the war on terror since 9/11 and, in a deeper historical perspective, to the West's political and military aggression against the Muslim world since at least the eleventh- to thirteenth-century Crusades; (c) partly premised on the availability of strong visual material with references to other injustices, most notably the Abu Ghraib photos; (d) anchored in a global Umma and based on solidarity with suffering Muslims everywhere, thus forming part of the *meaning infrastructure* of a global grievance community gravitating around the perceived unjust nature of the West's policies toward Muslims, Muslim societies, and the culture and religion of Islam. It was also noted how Guantanamo Bay is just one among a number of global injustice symbols employed by al-Qaeda and other actors within political Islam. Furthermore, it has been continuously underlined that political Islam as a political-cultural schema and grievance community cannot be reduced to the violent activism of al-Qaeda and other jihadist organizations. Yet al-Qaeda's employment of Guantanamo Bay merits particular attention due to their global visibility and ability to affect both Western security agendas and political-cultural agendas in the Muslim world. As repeatedly emphasized in chapter 1, the relationship between political actors and injustice symbols is a dialectical one. Al-Qaeda, from this perspective, is thus both producer and user of the Guantanamo Bay injustice symbol. What is notable about Guantanamo is that it had strong injustice symbolic potential from the outset by being so visibly located within the framework of the war on terror. Yet this potential had to be utilized by political actors. The transformation to symbolic status is always a result of interpretation and discursive efforts undertaken by activists and other political actors. In actively employing Guantanamo in their global communication efforts, al-Qaeda has transformed an empirical situation (or "object" in the vocabulary of chapter 1) into a symbol of a wider and essentially global problem: Western aggression, moral corruption, and disrespect for Islam as a whole. By thus infusing the empirical situation of Guantanamo with powerful injustice meanings, it becomes a symbolic resource that is available to and may be utilized for social and political ends by *other* actors in different places and in different times. Of course, Al-Qaeda has not done this single-handedly but in combination with a wider global social movement motivated by the Guantanamo Bay detention center.

Let us finally consider the implications of these observations for the overall theme of the book: the relationship between injustice symbols and global society. There are several themes to explore under this heading, but the following confines itself to two: the *contestedness* of the Guantanamo Bay injustice symbol and the *mutually productive* nature of injustice symbols. What is indicated by the contestedness of the Guantanamo Bay symbol is, among other things, the fact briefly alluded to earlier that this symbol not only belongs to al-Qaeda or even only actors within political Islam but it is also a recurrent and critical theme for *human rights* actors. For such actors, the detention center is problematic primarily because it constitutes and symbolizes the erosion of fundamental legal and political principles during the war on terror (e.g., Amnesty International, 2008, which tellingly refers to Guantanamo as a "wider symbol of injustice"). Allegations include the use of torture or torture-like interrogation techniques such as waterboarding. In the foreword to the organization's 2005 report, Secretary-General Irene Khan (2005) strongly condemned

Guantanamo Bay and what it stands for, referring to it as a gulag in order to emphasize the legal void in which it exists:

> the US government has gone to great lengths to restrict the application of the Geneva Conventions and to "re-define" torture. It has sought to justify the use of coercive interrogation techniques, the practice of holding "ghost detainees" (people in unacknowledged incommunicado detention) and the "rendering" or handing over of prisoners to third countries known to practice torture. The detention facility at Guantánamo Bay has become the gulag of our times, entrenching the practice of arbitrary and indefinite detention in violation of international law.

Recently, human rights activists have particularly targeted the above-mentioned decision to classify 48 detainees to be held at Guantanamo in indefinite detention. Human rights organizations have been continuously supported in their criticism by (some) states and international institutions. Speaking in the context of the 2013 hunger strikes at the facility, Navi Pillay (quoted in *Huffington Post*, 2013), UN high commissioner for human rights, said that "given the uncertainty and anxieties surrounding their prolonged and apparently indefinite detention in Guantanamo, it is scarcely surprising that people's frustrations boil over and they resort to such desperate measures." The criticism from human rights activists and international organizations focus strongly on the violation of international laws: "We must be clear about this: the United States is in clear breach not just of its own commitments, but also of international laws and standards that it is obliged to uphold. When other countries breach these standards, the U.S., quite rightly, strongly criticizes them for it" (Pillay, quoted in *Huffington Post*, 2013). Superficially, such arguments are not unlike those of al-Qaeda presented in the "Moral Corruption" subsection above. The difference, of course, lies in the political-cultural schemas from which these sets of arguments are derived. In other words, they are connected to wildly different interpretations and remedial visions. Human rights actors thus neither see the West and its political and cultural foundation as fundamentally flawed nor do they employ Guantanamo Bay to argument for violent action.

Furthermore, this conflict perspective is relevant for understanding how some symbols may be seen as *mutually and conflictively productive.* If we consider some of the major injustice symbols produced during the war against terrorism (especially, Guantanamo and Abu Ghraib), it makes sense to see them as closely related to another major injustice symbol: the 9/11 attacks and the iconic images associated with this event. "9/11" is a global injustice symbol, but one with particular resonance in the United States and those countries that consider themselves connected to the United States on a political and/ or cultural level. It now serves as a kind of *master injustice symbol* of the danger and immorality of violent jihadism and, to some extent, the political-cultural schema of political Islam. It achieved immediate symbolic status and was employed as a powerful tool in legitimating the war against terrorism. Today, more than ten years later, it remains an extremely powerful symbolic reference in politics in and outside of the United States. Thus, 9/11 is inseparable in an analytical sense from, for example, Guantanamo Bay and Abu Ghraib. Guantanamo was created to deal with combatants in the war against terrorism and, as such, is a direct and deliberate outcome of 9/11. The Abu Ghraib photographs, in contrast, were indirect and unintended outcome of this war, but nonetheless an injustice symbol intimately connected with the 9/11 events. Adding an additional layer of complexity, 9/11 itself is also an outcome of the past. The attack was motivated and legitimated by another powerful injustice symbol briefly touched upon in the chapter: Palestine. Thus, Palestine features, both before and after 9/11, as a central reference point in al-Qaeda's public interventions. It can be observed how sometimes injustice symbols *neutralize* each other. For some, for example, the injustice committed on 9/11 was justified in the light of the injustice committed in Palestine. For others, Guantanamo Bay is acceptable given its role in the struggle against terrorism and in light of the 9/11 injustice symbol. The power of one injustice symbol cancels or brackets another. Global society may be characterized by the availability and visibility of shared symbols. Yet as discussions of *contestedness* and *conflictive mutual production* indicate, this sharedness does not imply harmony or homogeneity. While a symbol such as Nelson Mandela (see chapter 2) is more or less surrounded by positive and unanimous interpretations, other symbols, such as Guantanamo Bay, Abu Ghraib, the Muhammad cartoons, and Palestine, are fiercely contested and interpreted from different and sometimes opposing political-cultural schemas and with reference, directly or indirectly, to other injustice symbols (these themes are taken up again in the concluding chapter 6).

# CHAPTER 4

# MORAL MEMORIES

As the world, over the summer of 1994, began to realize the scope and severity of the Rwandan genocide (most estimates today set the death toll between 500,000 and 1,000,000), accounts of the horrors were routinely followed by two questions: How could it happen and, then, how could *we* let it happen? The *moral shock* (see chapter 1) that the event triggered thus not only concerned the genocide itself but also the fact that the world had sat more or less idly by as men, women, and children were brutally and indiscriminately slaughtered over several months from April to July. As the violence subsided and the world's attention turned to the massive flood of refugees pouring into neighboring Zaire (now Democratic Republic of Congo), a process began that would gradually turn the Rwandan genocide into a global *moral memory*. Moral memories, broadly defined, are collectively developed and anchored memories that impinge, morally and politically, on the remembering collective. A *global* moral memory may, further, be defined as a local/national event/situation whose moral and political relevance has been expanded, or *spatiotemporally displaced* (see chapter 1), in such a way that it consistently occurs in political, moral, and cultural debates beyond its original spatial and temporal setting. Global society is a space traversed by moral memories: the Holocaust, My Lai, Tiananmen Square, and Srebrenica are just some of the most visible and best known such memories. Common for them all is that they stand out as cross-temporal carriers of values regarding unacceptable human behavior (as noted such claims are not only directed to the perpetrators but often to the spectators as well). There is a close relationship between moral memories and theme of this book: injustice symbols. In fact it might be argued that all injustice symbols, at least potentially, become moral memories as the temporal distance to the original event/situation widens. In other cases, the symbolization and memory process are closely intertwined in the sense that the object only acquires symbolic status at some temporal remove from the original event/situation. The latter seems to be the case with regard to the Rwandan genocide. While the lack of intervention, as noted above, became a topic immediately after the events, the symbolic status that the Rwandan genocide has today was gradually built up over the ensuing years.

The last two decades have seen a surge in memory research in a variety of academic fields (Olick, Vinitzky-Seroussi, and Levy, 2011). A number of scholars have applied the memory concept in global political sociology and international relations (Alexander, 2004c; Bell, 2006a; Edkins, 2003; Langenbacher and Shain, 2010; Levy and Sznaider, 2002; Müller, 2002; Olick, 2007; Zehfuss, 2007). Yet most of these works are characterized by a predominant focus on Europe and the United States. In them, for example, one only finds scattered references to what is arguably one of the major traumas and injustices of the recent past: the 1994 Rwandan genocide. Margalit (2002: 80) suggests that the intensity and visibility of memories depends on our cultural and geographic proximity to the original event. Thus, Margalit concludes, "Our memory of Kosovo overshadows our memory of Rwanda." It is, of course, difficult to ascertain with any certainty whether such an observation is empirically correct. However, the pace of the Rwandan genocide's transformation into a global moral memory and its repeated contemporary invocation and employment at least indicate that Margalit's indictment may be overly skeptical in regard to the potential of events outside the West becoming global moral memories.

Building on these arguments, the aim of the chapter is to identify and analyze the key elements in the transformation of the Rwandan genocide from a national event to global moral memory. This process has occurred within four interrelated areas: (a) at the *institutional* level, the tenth anniversary of the genocide sparked a Memorial Conference on the Rwanda Genocide at the UN and April 7 was declared the International Day of Reflection on the Genocide in Rwanda; (b) at the *moral* level, the Rwandan genocide has motivated widespread expressions of regret on the part of, in particular, states and international institutions; (c) at the *political* level, the Rwandan experience is recurrently invoked by organizations and individuals advocating intervention in, for example, Darfur; and (d) at the *cultural* level, the genocide has been made globally visible through numerous works of art (films, novels), documentaries, and journalistic accounts. The process leading to the formation of the Rwandan moral memory has been driven by a *global social movement* consisting of, as briefly illustrated above, various types of actors (see chapter 1) converging around the *political moralization* of the genocide. The chapter concludes with a discussion of the relevance of the Rwandan moral memory for our understanding of global society. This discussion will include a number of critical reflections on (a) how the global Rwandan memory involves the unremembering of or *amnesia* about certain aspects and (b) the global limitations and regional biases in the formation and employment of the memory.

## GLOBAL MORAL MEMORIES

The following section discusses global moral memories from a conceptual and theoretical perspective. It consists of five subsections: the first discusses the relevance of a global perspective on memories; the second distinguishes between three temporalities of moral memories; the third considers such memories from a universalization and responsibility perspective; the fourth looks at their employment in processes of analogical bridging; and the fifth focuses on the role of media in the formation of global moral memories.

### THE RELEVANCE OF GLOBAL MEMORIES

In 1990, Anthony D. Smith (1990: 118) formulated a powerful and still relevant counter-narrative to the ascending globalization paradigm. Smith did not deny the acceleration of globalizing dynamics in the fields of technology and economy but was adamant that these developments would not be paralleled by a global *culture* (see also Smith, 1995, for a later version of the argument): to believe that "'culture follows structure,' that the techno-economic sphere will provide the conditions and therefore the impetus and content of a global culture, is... to overlook the vital role of common historical experiences and memories in shaping identity and culture" (Smith, 1990: 180). To Smith, "a global culture is essentially memoryless... There are no *'world memories'* that can be used to unite humanity: the most global experiences to date—colonialism and the World Wars—can only serve to remind us of our cleavages" (179–180; emphasis added). While Smith's account remains a healthy antidote to heady hyper-globalist assertions about the erasure of nations and cultures in the era of globalization, it has the unfortunate effect of closing off important lines of sociological inquiry into global memories. In a well-known challenge to Smith, Levy and Sznaider (2002: 89) thus hold Smith's argument that nations are the only containers of culture to be "a breathtakingly unhistorical assertion." National culture and identity, they contend, are themselves historical constructs or inventions (Hobsbawn and Ranger, 1983)—imagined communities (Anderson, 1983) based on a forging (often in vehement opposition to local/regional identities) of new national identities and memories. There is no reason, Levy and Sznaider conclude, that similar processes could not evolve at the global level. While global culture and memories may not have the "thickness" and deep history of national cultures, this is insufficient to deny their relevance as emergent or potential phenomena. Levy and Sznaider offer the Holocaust experience as illustration. While they are cautious to remind us that the Holocaust memory does not mean the same to everyone everywhere, that its meaning is filtered, so to speak, through local and national specificities (2002: 92), they do assert that it has gradually attained the status of "a global collective memory" (93). Alexander (2004c: 197), in a similar vein, thus argues that the Holocaust "has come over the last fifty years to be redefined as a traumatic event for all of humankind," an event that "vividly 'lives' in the memories of contemporaries whose parents and grandparents never felt themselves even remotely related to it." The Holocaust example is

important because it challenges Smith's view that the World Wars I
and II only serve as memories of human division and suffering. While
the wars certainly convey this meaning, they cannot be reduced to it.
World War II, and in particular the Holocaust, led to a whole range
of normative and institutional (e.g., the 1948 creation of the Universal
Declaration of Human Rights) changes aimed at preventing human
suffering as a result of war and political persecution (Shaw, 2000:
122). This moral memory in human history thus continues to shape
contemporary political and *global* debates by offering yardsticks for
what we consider to be moral and immoral behavior (Alexander,
2004c: 249).

## THE THREE TEMPORALITIES OF MORAL MEMORIES

Collective memory becomes a central theme for political sociologists when the past is incorporated into contemporary (and future)
politics. This is particularly the case when a past event involves perceived injustices committed against groups or individuals: "Though
memory is concerned with past events, it is especially concerned with
those aspects of the past that remain unfinished business" (Poole,
2008: 160). The past is projected into the politics of the present: "It
is the project of memory to understand the past as a source of present
responsibilities" (Poole, 2008; see also Eyerman, 2004: 63; Booth,
2006: 118). Past events and situations of injustice are, consequently,
open social wounds that come to represent "a tear in the social fabric"
(Eyerman, 2004: 61): so even if injustices have been halted through
military intervention (as in the case of the Holocaust or Kosovo in
the late 1990s) or political pressure (as in the case of apartheid in
the 1980s), the atrocities already committed cannot be undone; they
linger on into the present and future with moral and political questions: What should we have done? Could we have done more? And
how do we prevent future injustices? (The issue of who constitutes the
"we" in these questions will be addressed in the next subsection, "The
Universalization of Moral Responsibility.") Memory processes involving past injustice thus contain a confluence of *three temporalities*: past,
present, and future. This finds expression in, for example, attempts

at institutionalizing past injustice. Three aspects, which are all revisited in the analysis of the Rwandan genocide below, characterize this process: first, in some cases, past injustices are anchored in the present through legal arrangements and institutions, for instance, criminal courts and national reconciliation processes (see, e.g., Goodman, 2011, for an analysis of The South African Truth and Reconciliation Commission; see also Torpey, 2003); second, the past may be reenacted in the present through commemorative days and events (e.g., Cubitt, 2007: 221; in 2005, for example, the UN designated January 27 as the International Holocaust Remembrance Day); third, the past is made available in the present in the form of memorial sites (e.g., Booth, 2006: 104; Nora, 1996; among the best-known sites in this category are the Holocaust memorial in Berlin, opened in 2005, and the Auschwitz-Birkenau memorial and museum). While these practices and institutions serve to provide past injustices with contemporary presence and visibility, they typically point to the future as well. As Booth (2006: 116) notes, the victims of the past issue "an unending appeal for justice" because the past cannot be altered. Yet even if this appeal is a gap that can never be filled, remembering is in most cases intimately tied to a *preventive* vision (never again!) in which the suffering and sacrifices have not happened in vain.

## THE UNIVERSALIZATION OF MORAL RESPONSIBILITY

The transformation of an event or situation to a collective memory or cultural trauma at its core involves *interpretive extension*. In the case of the Holocaust, Alexander (2004c: 197) writes, "This cultural transformation has been achieved because the originating historical event, traumatic in the extreme for a delimited particular group, has come over the last fifty years to be redefined as a traumatic event for all of humankind." This interpretive extension and psychological identification with the mass killings of Jews, Alexander (229) goes on, has "stimulated an unprecedented universalization of political and moral responsibility."[1] Alexander's argument about *universalization* is central to the concept of global moral memories. The questions that emanate from past injustices (see "Three Temporalities of Moral

Memories" subsection above) all invoke a moral "we." Remembering the past is about asserting who we are today and, it might be added, who we wish to be in the future. Alexander indicates that this moral and political "we" is increasingly defined in universal or global terms. Global moral memories are thus intimately connected to an implicit or explicit global "we" with moral responsibilities that extend beyond national boundaries and identities. This universalistic vision cannot be reduced to specific sets of actors; yet the intensification of universalistic conceptions of politics and morality in the post–World War II period coincides with the growth of global human rights activism (e.g., Anheier, Glasius, and Kaldor, 2001; Boli and Thomas, 1999; Sikkink and Smith, 2002). The majority of the world's largest human rights organizations thus advance a kind of double universalism: all people are endowed with the same set of basic rights and, resulting from this observation, the suffering of others, no matter where or who they are, thus becomes "our" moral and political concern.

### ANALOGICAL BRIDGING

Moral memories can enter into contemporary political debate in several ways. For a discussion of global moral memories, processes of *analogical bridging* (Alexander, 2004c: 247) are of particular interest. Analogical bridging occurs when a past event or situation is mobilized to underline the severity of a *present* event or situation in such a way as to legitimate a desired form of action. This highly flexible process may involve comparisons across both time and space. It is typically a variation over the following arguments: "This is just as terrible as the Holocaust"; "this is another My Lai";[2] or "if we don't do something now this will become as bad as Rwanda." In debates over possible intervention in the Balkan Wars, the Holocaust, for example, served as an analogical bridge (Alexander, 2004c: 247). This bridging was facilitated by certain iconic images. Central among these was the footage of a group of prisoners standing behind a barbed-wire fence at the Trnopolje camp in the Prijedor region. The center of the picture and subsequent attention was the prisoner Fikret Alic who appeared bare-chested and evidently emaciated (Campbell, 2002). The image invited immediate analogies to images of Jewish prisoners in Nazi concentration camps. The UK newspaper *Daily Mirror*, for example, ran a front cover on August 7, 1992, with the prisoner image and headlines proclaiming the camp as "Belsen 92" and the "Horror of the New Holocaust" (cited from Campbell, 2002). Similarly, even if apartheid no longer exists as a formal system of domination, its memory is frequently invoked beyond South Africa to highlight current situations of perceived injustice. Recently, critics of the Israeli West Bank barrier designed to prevent attacks emerging from the West Bank have described it as the Apartheid Wall, while others have portrayed contemporary global social and economic inequalities as a kind of global apartheid (e.g., Mutasa, 2004). Conway (2008: 198) offers a related analysis of the so-called Bloody Sunday where 13 civilians were killed by British military in Derry, Northern Ireland, in 1972. From the 1990s, Conway finds, Bloody Sunday was increasingly related to and compared with events and situations of injustice in places such as Palestine and Mexico. Such analogies may be superficial and sometimes even misplaced and factually wrong and therefore hotly contested (see, e.g., endnote 2 on the case of My Lai/Haditha). However, it should not lead us to overlook that analogical bridging is perhaps the primary way in which past injustices become part of global politics. The spatiotemporal *displacement* (see chapter 1) of the original event is vital to the formation of global moral memories and their insertion in the global public sphere.

## MEDIATED MEMORY

Collective memory work and rituals, as analyzed by Durkheim (1912/2001) in *The Elementary Forms of Religious Life*, is an ancient human activity. What distinguishes Durkheim's face-to-face communities from the modern period is that memory and identity processes increasingly occur at a distance and, as such, through the media (for a predominantly national perspective, see Anderson, 1983; Dayan and Katz, 1992). In a global context, Alexander's (2004c) above remarks on the universalization of a moral "we" indicate something important for this discussion: we tend to remember primarily those injustices that affect our own immediate identity groups or groups and individuals for whom we feel some kind of responsibility and solidarity attachment. It is precisely the expansion of the latter category that, from a sociological point of view, is the defining characteristic of political-cultural globalization. This is a process closely linked with, but not explained by, the increasing availability of images and information about distant events and suffering in the post–World War II period (Boltanski, 1999; Chouliaraki, 2006: Silverstone, 2007). The moral "we" is created based on a *global spectatorship* and what Jasper and Poulsen (1995; see also Jasper, 1997) call *moral shocks*. Moral shocks to a significant extent derive from powerful and disturbing images. The argument is relevant in the context of moral memories because the past is often remembered and ingrained in collective consciousness through iconic images and their ability to offer a very direct, and in a sense *un*mediated, emotional access to the suffering of others (Butler, 2010; Goldberg, 1991; Sontag, 2003). The vitality of Holocaust memories, for example, is deeply rooted in globally familiar images. Bodies being bulldozed into mass graves, the striped prisoner's garb used in most of the concentration camps, the despairing faces of emaciated men, women, and children staring at the viewer from "the other side" of both history and moral decency are all part of our shared knowledge of the Holocaust (Buettner, 2011). The Balkan Wars are similarly remembered through certain iconic images, in particular the Fikret Alic prison camp images discussed above (Campbell, 2002). The iconic status of this image was confirmed in the days following the arrest of Ratko Mladic (accused, among other things, of master minding the Srebrenica massacre) in May 2011. All over the world, broadcasters immediately retrieved this image from the archives to accompany news reports of Mladic's arrest. There is a second, *popular culture*, aspect of global spectatorship. To a significant extent, the Holocaust, for example, entered global collective memory through films, books, and biographies (Alexander, 2004c: 231–232). Another central moral memory of the modern period, antebellum American slavery, is similarly rooted in popular culture (Eyerman, 2004) and globally diffused through cultural products such as, for example, Alex Haley's *Roots* (the book, but not least the film) (and recently, *12 Years* *a Slave*). As noted by Alexander (2004b: 14), the transformation from event to collective trauma and memory is dependent on audience identification with the victims. Popular cultural renderings of suffering are thus typically shaped around individuals and families. The horrors of the large-scale events are personalized and made accessible to audiences in ways that facilitate *identification* and inclusion in the moral "we."

## THE 1994 RWANDAN GENOCIDE

The formation of the Rwandan genocide as a global moral memory is identifiable in four interrelated processes and domains that reflect core themes of the theoretical discussion above: (1) institutional legal arrangements and commemoration; (2) moral expressions of regret by third parties and bystanders; (3) analogical bridging; and (4) cultural production. This section opens with some reflections on methodology and an empirical background on the Rwandan genocide.

### A NOTE ON METHODOLOGY AND APPROACH

The analysis utilizes and blends a wide variety of empirical sources. Overall, the focus is on the discursive activities of actors making moral-political claims regarding the Rwandan genocide and, in particular, the responsibilities of non-Rwandan actors in relation to the genocide. Reflecting the argument in the introduction that the Rwandan memory process should be considered a global social movement, such activities are studied across several actor types: especially states, international institutions, activists, and the media. Since the moral memorization of the Rwandan genocide has taken place to a significant extent at a formal political level, the predominant focus is on states and international institutions (i.e., the UN). To support and supplement the focus on discursive activities, the research has also drawn on a number of other data sources, including legal documents, organizational documents, quantification of media coverage, and surveys of cultural productions. As in chapter 2 on Nelson Mandela and chapter 5 on Neda Agha Soltan, cultural productions are considered essential for the study of global injustice symbols (see chapter 1 for elaboration). The research process has also relied quite strongly on the vast literature on the Rwandan genocide that has emerged since 1994. While none of these works applies a perspective similar to this chapter, these works provide a number of crucial analytical insights and empirical information that has been integrated at several points in the chapter's analyses. The analyses are not chronologically structured, but rather thematically organized in four subsections following the "Background" subsection below. In all of the four analytical subsections, however, focus is on the period between 1994 and 2004, especially the period around the tenth anniversary in 2004 where the memory process peaked.

BACKGROUND

The Rwandan genocide had its roots in the ethnic division and tension between the Hutu (approximately 85% of the population) and Tutsi (approximately 15% of the population). From the late nineteenth century until the end of World War I, Rwanda was a German colony. The German colonizers ruled through the Tutsi monarchy and generally favored the Tutsi. Following World War I, Rwanda was acceded to Belgium, which continued the German policies of favoritism. The division between Hutu and Tutsi was cemented and institutionalized through identity cards labeling its holder as Hutu or Tutsi. After World War II, Hutus grew increasingly vociferous and political. In response, Belgium started changing the power structure in favor of the Hutus to contain the growing political unrest. As the power structure changed, violence between Hutus and Tutsis grew and thousands of Tutsis fled to neighboring countries. Violence continued after Rwanda gained its independence in 1962 and escalated into a civil war situation with exiled Tutsi military groups launching attacks on Rwandan territory. From 1973 to 1994, Rwandan politics was dominated by President Juvenal Habyarimana who effectively excluded the Tutsi from any share in political power. Under international pressure, Habyarimana signed a peace accord in 1993 that opened up to a transitory government that would include the main Tutsi political force, the Rwandese Patriotic Front (RPF). This move caused dissatisfaction among Hutu extremists. When President Habyarimana died in a plane crash on April 6, 1994 (the plane was shot down by as yet undetermined attackers), the political tension was almost immediately released into violence. The violence was instigated and carried out by Hutu extremists and, especially, by the Interahamwe, a paramilitary Hutu organization. Over the next 3 months between 500,000 and 1,000,000 million people, mainly Tutsis (but also moderate Hutus), were killed. With the signing of the peace accords in 1993, a UN peacekeeping force, United Nations Assistance Mission for Rwanda (UNAMIR), was established. Despite urgent calls from Roméo Dallaire (leader of the UNAMIR) for more troops to halt the violence, the UN and its member states acted slowly and not until the wave of violence had largely ceased. In parallel with the genocide, the Tutsi-dominated RPF gradually took control of Rwanda. The genocide ended with RPF's final takeover of power in July. This resulted in a massive flood of Hutu refugees to neighboring countries. The RPF has remained the dominant political force in Rwanda since 1994.

## INSTITUTIONALIZING THE RWANDAN GENOCIDE

In November 1994, the UN established the International Criminal Tribunal for Rwanda (ICTR) (UN, 1994). The aim of the tribunal is to prosecute individuals responsible for

> genocide and other serious violations of international humanitarian law committed in the territory of Rwanda and Rwandan citizens responsible for genocide and other such violations committed in the territory of neighboring States. (UN, 1994)

So far, the tribunal has completed 47 cases. At the time of writing (November 2013), another 16 cases are pending appeal. On July 1, 2012, the remaining cases of the ICTR were handed over to the International Residual Mechanism for Criminal Tribunals.[3] The creation of the tribunal by the Security Council and its location within the UN framework is an official "endorsement" by the community of states of the gravity of the Rwandan genocide (see also the section on "Regretting the Rwandan Genocide"). It is a signal to the world that the Rwandan genocide deserves special attention on a par with other large-scale atrocities followed by international tribunals (e.g., the Nuremburg Trials and the International Criminal Tribunal for the former Yugoslavia) and ingrained in global collective memory. By placing the Rwandan genocide in this specific historical category, the tribunal has enhanced its symbolic visibility across time and space. Furthermore, the institutionalization of the Rwandan genocide ensures that the genocide is provided a stable social and political presence in the present. Media reports during 1994 made the public painfully aware of the genocide. Media attention, however, is notoriously fleeting and focused on the immediate present. The media may provide the images and stories that generate public expectations for initiatives such as the establishment of the Rwandan tribunal, but can rarely be counted on to focus systematically on past events. The tribunal's proceedings provide a steady flow of newsworthy stories. When sentences are passed or new captives brought in, it prompts news stories that reenact the horrors.[4]

The tribunal's work is primarily aimed at the immediate perpetrators and ideological masterminds of the genocide. Its objective is to establish legal guilt so as to "contribute to the process of *national* reconciliation" (UN, 1994; emphasis added). Parallel to this legal and nationally oriented process, the Rwandan genocide has become the focal point of a set of global and officially sanctioned *commemoration* activities. Commemoration achieved a climax in 2004 at the tenth anniversary of the genocide when the governments of Canada and Rwanda organized a Memorial Conference on the Rwanda Genocide in New York. This commemoration had two interrelated purposes. First, it aimed at retrospectively honoring genocide victims. To this end, the UN General Assembly, on December 23, 2003, designated April 7 as the International Day of Reflection on the Genocide in Rwanda (UN, 2003). In his speech at the memorial conference, UN secretary-general Kofi Annan furthermore called for a minute of global silence to be observed on April 7. Second, in a broad and forward-looking political and moral vision, remembering the Rwandan genocide was integrated with affirmations of global collective responsibility: "May...we all reach beyond this tragedy, and work together to recognize our common humanity" (Annan, 2004; emphasis added).

The tribunal and commemoration activities mentioned above are located *outside* Rwanda. It is hardly surprising, however, that commemoration activities are most frequent and intense at the *national* level and in the *local* communities affected by the genocide. These are primarily centered around the Kigali Memorial Centre opened at the tenth anniversary of the genocide in April 2004. Despite its national anchoring, the memorial site has also played a key role in *global* memory formation. There are at least two global aspects to the site. First, it was set up and is run in cooperation between the Kigali city council and the UK-based civil society organization Aegis Trust and financed in part by the William Jefferson Clinton Foundation, the Swedish government, the Royal Embassy of the Netherlands, the Embassy of Belgium, and the United Kingdom's Department for International Development. Second, since the opening in 2004, the site has been visited by numerous politicians and celebrities. These include Paul Wolfowitz (then president of the World Bank), Ban Ki-moon (UN secretary-general), Nicholas Sarkozy (then president of France), Tony Blair (former prime minister of the United Kingdom), George W. Bush (then president of the United States), Horst Kohler (then president of Germany), and Didier Drogba (Ivory Coast national- and world-renowned football player) (Honore Gatera, Kigali Memorial Centre: personal correspondence, June 23, 2011).[5]

## REGRETTING THE RWANDAN GENOCIDE

Remembering injustice is a moral-political act that involves identifying perpetrators and victims. Such practices are often rooted in criminal tribunals, reconciliation and truth commissions (see Burnet, 2009, for an analysis of reconciliation politics in Rwanda after 1994), and reparation initiatives (see Vandeginste, 2003, for reparation in the case of Rwanda) and generally have a distinctly *national* character (this is the case even for international tribunals because their objective is primarily to assess guilt in relation to the conflicting parties). It is a key characteristic in the case of the Rwandan genocide and a major

factor in its transformation to global moral memory that these processes of guilt and responsibility have been expanded to third parties
and bystanders *beyond* Rwanda.

One of the earliest expressions of regret by a prominent decision
maker came in 1998 when US president Bill Clinton visited Rwanda:
"It may seem strange to you here...but all over the world there were
people like me sitting in offices, day after day after day, who did not
fully appreciate the depth and the speed with which you were being
engulfed by this unimaginable terror" (Clinton, 1998). Six years
later, at the tenth anniversary of the genocide, Kofi Annan's remarks
(2004) similarly gravitated around the responsibility of the UN and
the international community: "The genocide in Rwanda should never,
ever have happened. But it did. The international community failed
Rwanda, and that must leave us always with a sense of bitter regret
and abiding sorrow." For both Clinton and Annan, guilt was not only
placed at an institutional or structural level but also personalized: "I
believed at that time that I was doing my best. But I realized after the
genocide that there was more that I could and should have done to
sound the alarm...This painful memory...has influenced much of
my thinking" (Annan, 2004). Apart from these high-profile expressions of regret and guilt, official apologies have been made by the
Belgian government, the European Union, and the African Union
(Grünfeld and Huijboom, 2007: ch. 18). Most apologies have come
in the context of the tenth anniversary, which in this sense, as noted
above, represents the pivotal moment in the transformation of the
genocide into a global moral memory. The backgrounds for these
apologies reflect different circumstances but are all to some extent
grounded in the discrepancy between the amount and severity of
early warnings and calls for intervention immediately before and during the genocide and the weak response by states and international
institutions (see Grünfeld and Huijboom, 2007, for a detailed analysis
of the information available before and during the genocide; see also
the discussion of Romeo Dallaire in the "Dramatizing the Rwandan
Genocide" section below).[6]

The injustice related to the Rwandan memory thus attains two
meanings. The genocide constitutes an injustice in and by itself (this

is the aspect dealt with by the criminal tribunal for Rwanda); yet it also concerns sins of omission on the part of those *outside* of Rwanda, primarily international institutions and states deemed to have had, but not used, their military and political capacity for intervention (e.g., the United States and France), who watched and knew (at least partly) without committing to decisive action. As mentioned in the introduction, the question "how could it happen" has been routinely complemented by another, "how could *we* let it happen?" The fact that responsibility has been so powerfully expanded to encompass third parties in a spectatorship position (the "we") is perhaps the most vivid testament to the global character of the Rwandan moral memory.

### EVOKING THE RWANDAN GENOCIDE

The preceding subsection discussed how the memory of the Rwandan genocide is active in the present because the issue of moral and political responsibility keeps reverberating. Through the institutional arrangements discussed earlier and the continued cultural and political interest in Rwanda, the issue of, in particular, Western reluctance to intervene remains a prominent theme globally. Over time, however, these discussions have been paralleled by a tendency to employ the Rwandan memory in relation to *other* events and situations that may bear some resemblance to the Rwandan genocide prior to or during the genocide in 1994. Analogical bridging of this kind is key evidence of the transformation from event to memory, suggesting that the event has reached symbolic maturity and been established as an interpretive frame with wide global availability.

There is no doubt that Darfur would have emerged as a topical theme in the absence of the Rwandan experience. Yet, it is highly probable that the intensification of the Rwandan memory at the tenth anniversary in 2004 helped expose and draw global attention to atrocities in Darfur. When, for example, US secretary of state Colin Powell somewhat controversially chose to classify the situation in Darfur as genocide in 2004 (Kessler and Lynch, 2004), the definition and its public and political credibility owed considerably to the already existing Rwandan frame.[7] And in a speech to the Commission on Human

Rights on April 7, 2004 (the International Day of Reflection on the Genocide in Rwanda), Kofi Annan used the occasion to underline the severity of the situation in Darfur, stating how it left him "with a deep sense of foreboding" (Annan, 2004). While politicians and institutional representatives such as Powell and Annan have been active in analogical bridging of the Rwandan genocide and Darfur, the most vociferous claims in that regard have been made by human rights organizations and the media. In the wake of the tenth anniversary of the Rwandan genocide, Human Rights Watch (2004) had a clear message for the world's politicians: "Ten years after the Rwandan genocide and despite years of soul-searching, the response of the international community to the events in Sudan has been nothing short of shameful." In the analysis of many human rights organizations, it appears that the "apologies" of politicians and officials are not sincere or at least lack real political will to convert the memory of the Rwandan genocide into decisive action in present Darfur. The hesitations regarding Darfur testify to the sense that despite assurances nothing has fundamentally changed. Speaking in the context of the Rwandan genocide's commemorations in April 2004, the International Crisis Group (Evans and Ellis, 2004) linked the Rwandan genocide (as well as a string of other atrocities and human rights violations) to Darfur in a somewhat disillusioned analysis:

> It's time this week to remember all this; and to say once more . . . "never again". But these are the same words we uttered after the Holocaust; and after the Cambodian genocide in the 1970s; and, barely a year later than Rwanda, after the genocidal massacre at Srebrenica. (Evans and Ellis, 2004)

Each time these atrocities happen, the organization claims, "We look back wondering, with varying degrees of incomprehension, horror, anger and shame, how we could have let it all happen. And then we let it happen all over again." The same tone was encountered on the editorial pages of newspapers around the world in the years following the tenth anniversary of the Rwandan genocide. Referring to Darfur, the *New York Times* (2004) provided a straight analogical bridge to the Rwandan genocide in a June 2004 editorial: "Bush administration lawyers are busily studying whether this meets the legal definition of genocide, but that misses the point." What is important, the editorial goes on, is that "the rising death toll could soon evoke memories of the tragedy in Rwanda a decade ago, when both the United States and the Security Council found excuses to stand aside while 800,000 died. That shameful failure must not be repeated" (see also Beardsley, 2009; Caplan, 2009; Grzyb, 2009, for academic and critically motivated analyses comparing the Rwandan genocide and Darfur). As the quotes above demonstrate, it is in analogical bridging processes that the *political* aspects of memory work are most evident. The invocation in the last three quotes of the term "shame" is used as a springboard to demand the kind of intervention in Darfur that was absent in the Rwandan genocide. The moral wound of the past is made politically active in the present and projected into the future. Memory, in other words, is not enough:

> Something more than memory is needed if another catastrophic genocide is not to happen...We have to pay constant attention to high-risk situations...have the political commitment to act if circumstances cry out for it; and have available the necessary resources to make that commitment effective. (Evans and Ellis, 2004)

The Rwandan genocide (the past) is analogically bridged with, for example, Darfur (the present), while both events are key motivations for setting up preventive mechanisms for (future) atrocities considered to be inevitable. Commemoration and respect for the victims of the past are intimately linked with the politics of both present and future: "Therefore, as the only fitting memorial the United Nations can offer to those whom its inaction in 1994 condemned to die...I wish today to launch an Action Plan to Prevent Genocide" (Annan, 2004).

### DRAMATIZING THE RWANDAN GENOCIDE

A key argument of this chapter is that events do not become moral memories solely or primarily through political and institutional activities such as the ones analyzed in the preceding sections. Only when these activities occur in parallel with the emergence of cultural products may we consider the event to be entering into collective memory.

It is a vital testament to the resonance of the Rwandan genocide that the list of art works (films, books, photography, plays, exhibitions, etc.) related to this event is too long to be reproduced here. The following discussion primarily focuses on the genre that has generated the most public visibility in the cultural arena: docudrama films. In the time around the tenth anniversary of the genocide, three major films appeared: *Hotel Rwanda* (2004/2005, the United States, directed by Terry George), *Shooting Dogs* (2005, the United Kingdom and Germany, directed by Michael Caton-Jones), and *Sometimes in April* (2005, France and the United States, directed by Raul Peck).[8] All three films offer dramatized renditions of the genocide structured around authentic personal stories. *Hotel Rwanda*, for example, tells the story of a Rwandan hotelier, Paul Rusesabagina (played by Don Cheadle), who tries to shelter his family and several hundred refugees at the Hôtel des Mille Collines, while the central character (played by John Hurt) in *Shooting Dogs* is built on Bosnian Croat priest Vjeko Curic's attempt to protect genocide refugees in his parish.[9] While all focus on personal dramas and less on the national and international political dimensions of the genocide, the films and their reception are cultural-*political* in at least two senses. First, while reviews discuss the artistic qualities of the films, the political and moral aspects outlined in the preceding sections are typically incorporated in them at some level: "In retrospect, it's mind-boggling that the rest of the world did nothing as 800,000 people were murdered in Rwanda in a bizarre case of ethnic strife between Hutu and Tutsi Rwandans" (Hornaday, 2005: review of Hotel Rwanda in *Washington Post*). Second, the films have been used in connection with public social and political activities. In an event on January 31, 2007, Aegis, a British organization working on genocide-related issues (and centrally involved in the Kigali Memorial Centre), for example, screened *Shooting Dogs* in the context of a panel discussion on Darfur (Aegis, 2007).

The very production and favorable global reception of these films at some temporal distance from the genocide, on the one hand, indicate how the Rwandan genocide is *already* integrated in global collective memory. On the other hand, they serve to further *strengthen* this status. The power of cultural products, and perhaps especially films, in the formation of collective moral memories has three aspects: first, films have the capacity of reaching audiences who do not follow foreign event news on a regular basis; second, when they appear significantly after the original events, they are able to transpose the memory to those who were children, adolescents, or not born at the time; and third, films, through their combination of dramatization and images, have the ability to help us remember through emotions rather than objective facts. "It's one thing to know, in an abstract, intellectual sort of way that between 500,000 and 850,000 moderate Hutus and Tutsis were slaughtered in the space of three months," but it is "quite another to see the bloody handprints on the wall left by those scrabbling to escape as grenades were lobbed into packed classrooms" (Wrong, 2005; review and analysis of four Rwandan-genocide-related films in *Guardian*).

As in the case of art works, the list of books and documentaries produced for popular public debate is comprehensive.[10] Prominent in this category is *Shake Hands with the Devil: The Failure of Humanity in Rwanda* by Roméo Dallaire (2003). The book's special status is caused by the fact that Roméo Dallaire, a Canadian lieutenant general, was stationed in Rwanda during the genocide as part of the UNAMIR mission.[11] Dallaire attained near-iconic status (underlining the point made in chapter 1 that symbols often occur within symbolic families) as it gradually became evident how he had struggled in vain to have the UN and key states commit to intervention, while at the same time staying on in Rwanda despite orders to withdraw. The publication of the book coincided with the tenth anniversary of the genocide and received widespread acclaim and attention throughout the world. Dallaire's book added significantly to the already established analysis that the world, and in particular the UN and key states such as the United States and France, had failed Rwanda. Dallaire's book and his global reputation has made him an active and sought after commentator on the Darfur crisis. In a tellingly titled and analogically bridging op-ed in *New York Times*, "Looking at Darfur, Seeing Rwanda,"

Dallaire (2004) expressed considerable pessimism despite US and UN suggestions to impose trade sanctions on Sudan and expand African Union forces on the ground: "But I am afraid that moral condemnation, trade penalties and military efforts by African countries are simply not going to be enough to stop the killing—not nearly enough. I know, because I've seen it all happen before."

## CONCLUSION

Within a relatively short span of time, and culminating with the tenth anniversary of the genocide in 2004, the 1994 Rwandan genocide has become a key global moral memory. This is evident in the way its formation and continued prominence traverses several domains (institutional, moral, political, and cultural) and involves actors from the formal political system, civil society, and the media in several countries and at the global level.

The defining feature of a *global* (as opposed to local or national) moral memory is that the reference event is (a) systematically addressed and invoked in societies outside its original national and regional context, (b) formally and informally recognized by international bodies such as international institutions and human rights organizations, and (c) infused with moral and political implications that involve third parties and bystanders beyond the national and regional setting of the original events. Concerning point (a), this aspect is primarily evident in two areas: first, in the way the Rwandan genocide has been used as an analogical bridge in, especially, Darfur-related debates in societies all over the world; and, second, in the extent to which the Rwandan genocide has become a source for art work (e.g., films) and popular-debate products (e.g., journalistic and eyewitness books/documentaries) outside Rwanda. Concerning point (b), the genocide has received *formal* recognition as a major injustice through the creation of an international criminal tribunal and international commemoration activities (the use of the term "international," rather than global, denotes how these institutions and activities are state initiatives). At a more informal level, the genocide is recognized as a major injustice by large and globally oriented and organized human rights organizations such as Amnesty International and Human Rights Watch. This recognition is expressed, partly, through the analogical bridging activities also mentioned in relation to point (a). Concerning point (c), this aspect will be covered below.

Two observations make the Rwandan genocide a global *moral/ injustice* memory. First, the killing of between 500,000 and 1,000,000 people, among them many women, children, and elderly, is obviously in itself a glaring injustice. Second, it seems reasonable to suggest that the rise of the Rwandan genocide to the global level considerably results from the fact that this injustice was expanded, as it were, beyond Rwanda. Whether we look at the institutional, moral, political, or cultural aspects of the Rwandan genocide memory, the haunting question appears to be not only "how could it happen" but equally "how could *we* let this happen." The latter question was made legitimate when it emerged that key persons in the UN (e.g., Kofi Annan) and in leading states (e.g., Bill Clinton and the United States) had received warning signs and information (in particular from Roméo Dallaire) about the impending and unfolding genocide but did not devise effective strategies to seriously affect the events. The fact that indirect blame and moral condemnation could thus be plausibly turned toward third parties and bystanders means that the local/ national injustice of the genocide has been increasingly globalized. Such an analysis was present from the first months after the genocide and delivered by politicians, media, activist organizations, artists, and commentators alike but slowly grew to culminate at the tenth anniversary commemorations.

To speak about the Rwandan genocide as a global injustice *memory* raises at least two interrelated questions: (a) When does an event become a memory rather than merely a historical occurrence, and (b) in relation to the Rwandan genocide, is this event not still too young to be considered a memory in the same league as, for example, the Holocaust, My Lai, and some of the other injustice events discussed above? Concerning point (a), the transformation from event to memory requires some element of institutionalization and formalization. For this reason, the tenth anniversary in 2004 of the genocide and the formal recognition activities related to it have been prominent in the chapter. Of course, this is not to suggest that events cannot be considered memories in the absence of such activities. Rather, it may be useful to think of memories with varying intensity and visibility. The highest level of memory intensity and visibility is achieved when formal (institutionalization) and informal (e.g., expressions of regret, analogical bridging, cultural production) activities combine, as in the Rwandan genocide's case. Regarding point (b), the commemoration activities at the tenth anniversary and the continued presence of the genocide in contemporary processes of analogical bridging and cultural products suggest that the event is now so firmly established in the collective consciousness that it may reasonably be considered a fully developed moral memory. Rather, the thornier question is whether the Rwandan memory has survived beyond the tenth anniversary with the same degree of intensity. There is no doubt that the anniversary represented a climax, not only as expressed in the formal activities described above but also in the host of informal activities that coincided with them. Yet the Rwandan memory remains present, if perhaps at a lower level of intensity: prominent non-Rwandans continue to visit the memorial center in Kigali; convictions at the criminal court still receive attention in media around the world; activist organizations recurrently employ the Rwandan genocide in analogical bridging processes; and there is a steady trickle of films, books, and documentaries addressing the genocide.

Finally, a couple of remarks that in different ways problematize the Rwandan memory in relation to the book's broader discussion of global society are in place. *First*, it should be made clear that even if the Rwandan memory is indeed global, it is not global in the sense that it is equally appreciated, known, and interpreted across the globe. Aksu (2009: 328–329) and Bell (2006b: 18) are skeptical of the term "global memory" precisely for these reasons. We might suggest, accordingly, that the Rwandan memory is quite unevenly distributed, nationally as well as regionally. Because the genocide was seen as a moral and political failure for key states in the West (especially France and the United States) and because the events took place in Africa, memories of the genocide are undoubtedly more firmly rooted in these regions of the world. Furthermore, as indicated with this observation, the Rwandan memory is much more firmly established in some countries than in others. To mention just one example, the French parliament in 1998 initiated hearings intended to map the degree of responsibility among French officials and ministers at the time of the genocide (Whitney, 1998). France's preoccupation with the genocide stemmed from its historically strong role in Africa and, more importantly, allegations that French military had trained and advised the Interahamwe, a Hutu militia responsible for a large part of the killings during 1994. This leads to the *second* point to be emphasized here. Remembering, and symbol formation in general, is a human process of meaning infusion, as argued in chapter 1. It follows from this observation that it is also a selective and potentially excluding process in the sense that the memory/symbol is infused with *certain* meanings and, hence, not others. The dominant analytical story told in this chapter concerns how something *they* did became *our* concern because of the surrounding world's lack of attention and intervention. While key non-Rwandan actors have thus administered significant blame on themselves, this process seems to have involved, at least at the official level, an unremembering of or amnesia about the fact that the conditions of interethnic conflict that fueled the genocide were at least partly a result of Western (and especially Belgian) colonialist policies during the nineteenth and twentieth centuries, which amplified ethnic differences and tensions for political reasons (e.g., Melvern, 2000). Remembering, in other words, is also to some extent *forgetting*. The wider implications of these insights for the understanding and analysis of global society are addressed in chapter 6.

# CHAPTER 5

# DRAMATIC DIFFUSION

WHEN 26-YEAR-OLD NEDA AGHA SOLTAN WENT INTO THE STREETS of Tehran to protest fraudulent presidential elections on June 20, 2009, she was just one among thousands of aggrieved Iranians. At the end of that day, however, she had been catapulted to the global public sphere and transformed into a *symbol* of political repression in Iran. At some point during the protests, Neda was hit and killed by a gunshot. The scene that followed, in which we see Neda collapsing and bleeding profusely, was recorded on a bystander's cell phone and fed into global communicative networks. Within hours, the footage had been *dramatically diffused* worldwide, generating a *global social movement* of shocked reactions from a wide range of actors. The dramatic diffusion of Neda's shooting exemplifies the role and power of what might be labeled as *violent person-events* in generating political action, locally, nationally, and globally. In recent years, such events have been at the center of political protest in several countries and on a global scale: for example, Khaled Said, beaten to death by Egyptian police in 2010 (Olesen, 2013b); Mohamed Bouazizi, who set himself on fire in a protest against local authorities in Tunisia in 2010 (Lim, 2013); Malala Yousafzai, shot and severely injured by the Taliban because of her advocacy for girls' right to education in Pakistan in 2012; and Jyoti Singh, who died after being gang raped on a Delhi bus in 2012. The case of Neda also points to the potential political power of *images* and *amateur journalism*. In the present situation, events in public space are increasingly subject to documentation by citizens who, often by chance, come to act as amateur journalists, providing information with strong political content and potential. The extension and efficiency of *global communicative networks* enable such information to be circulated rapidly and at almost no cost. Following from the preceding points, the case of Neda (and other violent person-events) and her dramatic global diffusion illustrates a process of *scale shift* (Tarrow, 2005). Violent person-events are thus, at the outset, always local and/or national. Shifting scale to the global level, the violent person-event is confronted with new audiences who are likely to interpret the event in different ways than local and national audiences. Dramatic diffusion in this sense necessarily involves some degree of change and *adaptation* in the way violent person-events are interpreted and infused with meaning.

The chapter aims to balance all these analytical lines (images, amateur journalism, global communication networks, and meaning adaptation) but refracts them mainly through the theme of *meaning adaptation*. While the chapter, as noted above, points to intensification in both the potential and reality of dramatic cross-border diffusion, the adaptation perspective attempts to provide an antidote to the sometimes rather loose and optimistic cosmopolitanism associated with such analyses. It does so by arguing that meaning adaptation and global symbol formation occurs through existing dominant *political-cultural schemas* available at the level of global society. These schemas shape the content of injustice symbols in ways that reflect the values and agendas of their sponsors. This is a dialectical process, however. On the one hand, as the term "adaptation" indicates, local/national violent person-events are shaped to resonate with existing schemas. On the other, schemas are not static but develop in constant interaction with the empirical phenomena to which they provide meaning. In the present chapter, this argument is employed to shed analytical and critical light on the political-cultural interchange between the North and the South. It is thus notable that most violent person-events attaining global resonance originate in the South (this theme is also addressed in chapter 6). Yet, their passage into the global public sphere and their transformation into global injustice symbols are often premised on some degree of adaptation to largely Western-based schemas. While thi s obser-vation constitutes a significant line of analysis in the chapter, adap-tation is not simply seen as a question of *meaning reduction* and of non-Western violent person-events being forced into a Western mold (e.g., Said, 1978; Spivak, 1988). Western conceptions about the non-West are also, at least potentially, challenged, nuanced, and expanded (Chabot and Duyvendak, 2002; Olesen, 2005). In the present chapter, it is argued that the Neda injustice symbol was globally shaped in interaction with a globally available political-cultural schema that casts Iran as a *political other* of the West (i.e., representing what we are *not*). The analysis consists of two main sections followed by a concluding section. The first section outlines Iran's political-cultural schema. The second focuses on the process of symbol formation through three lenses: the location of Neda in a global history of democratic struggles; the Iranian regime's attempts at de-symbolization, which for many confirmed the validity of the Iranian schema; and the role and power of images in the dramatic diffusion of Neda.

## DRAMATIC CROSS-BORDER DIFFUSION

The following offers a theoretical discussion of the core concepts of the chapter in four subsections. The first locates the concept of dramatic diffusion in the wider literature on social movement diffusion. The second develops the concept of violent person-events and its relation to injustice symbols. The third outlines the different trajectories and actors engaged in dramatic diffusion. The fourth discusses meaning adaptation as a central element in processes of dramatic diffusion.

### VIOLENCE AND DIFFUSION

While the concept of diffusion is a central focus of the chapter, the approach taken here differs quite significantly from the existing lit-erature on movement-related cross-border diffusion (e.g., Beissinger, 2007; Chabot, 2010; Chabot and Duyvendak, 2002; McAdam and Rucht, 1993; Snow and Benford, 1999; Tarrow, 2005). The issue of adaptation is also a staple in the existing literature on cross-border movement diffusion. Snow and Benford (1999: 30), for example, define it as "the strategic appropriation of specific foreign elements that adopting agents modify, for their own purposes, in a fashion congruent with the host culture's values, beliefs, and practices." The existing literature, as exemplified in the quote, thus typically works with a clearly defined and strategically oriented sender-recipient relationship and with concrete items being diffused across space. The dramatic cross-border diffusion perspective differs in at least two ways. First, the item diffused in dramatic cross-border diffusion is not a social movement slogan, repertoire, or tactic, a focus predominant throughout the existing literature (e.g., Beissinger, 2007; Chabot and Duyvendak, 2002) but rather a violent person-event (this element motivates the adjective "dramatic"). Second, the recipient in diffusion processes is typically a social movement. In the case of dramatic cross-border diffusion, the recipient aspect is more complex, as will be evident in the analysis. Those actors who receive or engage with violent person-events may, of course, include social movements and activists, but in line with the broad definition of global social movements proposed in chapter 1, may also include the media, politicians and political parties, institutions, and networked citizens. Dramatic cross-border diffusion may thus, in sum, be defined in two interrelated tracks as (a) *the cross-spatial spread of knowledge about violent person-events* (through a combination of written, oral, and visual documentation) and (b) *the moral-political reactions to this documentation from actors outside the local and/or national location of the event* (the combination of knowledge spread and reaction/resonance is elaborated below). It is argued that when these two elements combine in a specific temporal sequence, it constitutes a global social movement.

## Violent Person-Events

Violent person-events form the empirical basis (the object; see chapter 1) of what might be thought of as *individual injustice symbols* (as opposed, for example, to injustice symbols based on collective events such as massacres). To become an object in the process of injustice symbolization, the victims of violence must be considered innocent, decent, and thus undeserving of violence. Individual injustice symbols thus contain two basic empirical elements or objects: a specific individual and the violence that this individual has suffered. The sum of these parts is referred to here as a *violent person-event*. A violent person-event does not automatically become an injustice symbol but only constitutes its "material" basis. Violent person-events have the potential to arouse *moral shock* (Jasper, 1997; Jasper and Poulsen, 1995) in an audience. Moral shocks can have various sources: for example, as suggested above, it can be derived from violence against individuals with pronounced innocence status (e.g., children; Sznaider, 2001); from graphic visual documentation of violence (Alexander, Bartmanski, and Giesen, 2012; Hariman and Lucaites, 2007; Zelizer, 2010) acquired by professional journalists or amateur journalists (Greer and McLaughlin, 2010); and from the character of the violence (e.g., torture and mutilation). Preparing a violent person-event for injustice meaning infusion thus involves the presentation of credible information about the circumstances of the event and some knowledge about the victim of violence. Ideally, this exercise is able to establish injustice and innocence (these and following points are pertinent to individual injustice symbol formation at both the local/national and global level). In the case of Mohamed Bouazizi whose self-immolation in 2010 was a triggering event in the Tunisian Revolution in Tunisia, it thus became crucial (a) why he self-immolated and (b) who he was *before* his decision to self-immolate. Bouazizi self-immolated after a clash with local authorities over his right to sell goods at the market in Sidi Bouzid. It was vital for the establishment of innocence that Bouazizi had not been the aggressor in the clash with authorities. While there was a heated argument in which Bouazizi resisted authority demands, the police and municipal officers were subsequently portrayed as aggressors. Initial accounts thus claimed that a female municipal officer, Faida Hamdi, had slapped Bouazizi in the face (but as will be discussed in endnote 2, this account was later contested significantly). But innocence was also asserted in a more indirect sense. The incident triggering Bouazizi's act thus happened in a wider social and political context. While street vending was probably not his preferred career choice, it was one of the few options available to him in a context of pronounced youth unemployment in Tunisia. Bouazizi, in other words, was (or, rather, could be claimed to be) a victim of adverse structural conditions: a sluggish economy, extreme youth unemployment, and a culture of corruption. It was thus the confluence of these factors on December 17, 2010, embodied in the altercation between Bouazizi and municipal authorities, that pushed Bouazizi to end his life in such a drastic and abrupt fashion. Descriptions emerging in the wake of December 17 told of a hardworking man struggling as a single provider for his mother, stepfather, and five siblings. Bouazizi's father had died when Bouazizi was three years old (Ryan, 2011). His mother later remarried but his stepfather was unable to provide for the family due to health reasons. Bouazizi had a huge responsibility on his shoulders and had it since a young age (according to his mother he started working in the market at the age of 12; de Soto, 2011). In the context of extremely high numbers of youth unemployment in Tunisia (in 2008, it was nearly 30% for age groups below 30 years; Haouas, Sayre, and Yagoubi, 2012: 401), he had set up his own small business in the informal economy sector to make ends meet.[1] Working outside the legal realm, Bouazizi and his fellow street vendors were routinely harassed by police and municipal officers and forced to pay bribes in order to maintain the right to work in the street. Bouazizi appears to have been well liked and respected by his peers in the market (de Soto, 2011). According to a friend, Hajlaoui Jaafer, "What really gave fire to the revolution was that Mohamed was a very well-known and popular man" (quoted in Ryan, 2011). Thus, the image left behind by Bouazizi was one of an honest, respected, and responsible young man trying to lead a dignified life and provide for his family in adverse conditions. Just as credible accusations of mental instability would have decreased the political power of his self-immolation, the presence of character flaws such as laziness and irresponsibility would have significantly limited Bouazizi's potential as an injustice symbol.[2]

Often, the violence involved in violent person-events and the formation of individual injustice symbols is committed by state authorities, such as military or police, but perpetrators may also be non-state actors (e.g., the case of Malala Yousafzai in Pakistan, 2012), fellow citizens (e.g., the case of Jyoti Singh in India, 2012), and even the individual him or herself (the case of Mohamed Bouazizi). What is decisive, then, for injustice symbol formation is not (only) the perpetrator but rather whether the violent person-event has universalizing potential (Alexander, 2006), that is, can be linked to a social, cultural, and/or political problematic with structural roots. In the case of Malala Yousafzai, for example, her shooting was immediately connected to the gender politics of radical Islamists.

## ACTORS AND TRAJECTORIES

The qualities and characteristics of violent person-events mentioned above (innocence, decency) only create a *potential* for individual injustice symbol formation. Countless violent person-events meet these criteria without becoming injustice symbols. The formation of injustice symbols requires *agency*. We cannot in other words expect to explain the formation of individual injustice symbols only by pointing to the intrinsic "qualities" of the individual and the event. The main agents in the formation of individual injustice symbols are political activists, the media, and networked citizens. While driven by different logics (Gamson and Wolfsfeld, 1993; Rucht, 2004), media and activists often interact, if rarely intentionally and planned, in the production of individual injustice symbols (Greer and McLaughlin, 2010). For political activists, acts of violence against innocent individuals offer important opportunities to dramatize and publicly expose issues already on their agenda. For the media, violence against individuals corresponds with established news criteria such as conflict, drama, and personalization (e.g., Bennett, 1983/2005). In the present situation where citizens are easily and constantly connected to global communicative networks, individuals may acquire political agency roles by forwarding and/or commenting on violent person-events in and through their personal networks. Obviously these types of agencies often interact. Sometimes dramatic diffusion may be initiated by media reports and photojournalism; in other cases it is initiated by activists or networked citizens who have gathered or received information and documentation, which is then seized by the media. In some cases, agency of this kind occurs in a paradoxical interaction with perpetrators or actors considered directly or indirectly responsible for the violence. A key dynamic in this relationship is what Hess and Martin (2006) refer to as *backfire*. In other words, injustice symbol formation may be facilitated by responsible actors' attempt to de-symbolize violence by denying, concealing, or manipulating the event. The "backfire" term is relevant because such acts often serve to amplify the victim's innocence.

Inspired by Koopmans (2004), dramatic cross-border diffusion and individual injustice symbol formation can be analytically broken down into the two phases suggested earlier (knowledge/visibility and reaction/resonance). According to Koopmans, a political message can achieve public visibility through media attention. Visibility, however, does not guarantee resonance—that other actors react to the message. This terminology may be applied to the present purpose as follows: cross-border diffusion of a violent person-event primarily involves the creation of global *visibility*, that is, making the event known to audiences outside its original spatial context. Yet, global injustice symbol formation only occurs if morally and politically indignant actors outside this context adopt and critically engage with the diffused event to generate *resonance*. Dramatic cross-border diffusion generally follows one of two ideal typical trajectories. In some cases (referred to in chapter 1 as the step pattern), the violent person-event has already, wholly or partly, attained injustice symbolic status at the local/national level (as in the cases of Jyoti Singh and Mohamed Bouazizi). In other cases (referred to in chapter 1 as the circumvention pattern), diffusion circumvents the local/national level, feeding more or less directly into the global public sphere (this, as we shall see shortly, characterizes the case of Neda Agha Soltan). Activists, media, and networked citizens play central roles as diffusers in dramatic cross-border diffusion. These may usefully be divided into two categories: in a dynamic resembling the so-called boomerang pattern (Keck and Sikkink, 1998), local/national actors may seek to promote the violent person-event globally in order to activate pressure on local and national authorities (see also Bob, 2005); or actors from outside the local/national context who have an interest in the relevant country and/or the issue represented by the violent event may use it to promote their agenda in their own national setting or at a global level (addressing, for example, international institutions).

## MEANING ADAPTATION

As noted earlier, resonance and symbol formation occur when actors outside the original spatial context adopt and critically engage with the violent person-event. Adoption and critical engagement typically involves a degree of *adaptation* where the adopter construes the issue according to their worldview and belief systems. In this way, global injustice symbols not only point to the victim and his/her context but also say something important about the adopter and their moral and political self-understanding (see also chapter 2 on Nelson Mandela for a related point). What is of interest, then, is the meaning process through which an empirical violent person-event is transformed into a symbolic end product. This process occurs in and through existing *political-cultural schemas* available in the global public sphere (see chapter 1). A schema provides meaning to and orients the understanding of empirical events. The schemas employed in the formation of global injustice symbols are always critical in the sense that they contain and point to purported conditions of injustice. Schemas are not static but "ebb and flow in prominence and are constantly revised and updated to accommodate new events" (Gamson and Modigliani, 1989: 2). While the symbolization of violent person-events is a process shaped by existing schemas, it does not necessarily imply reduction in a negative sense (the scope and character of adaptation can only be empirically and not theoretically answered). Through the process of adaptation, the event and the symbolic outcome becomes integrated in, and thus potentially changes, the political-cultural schema.

### THE DEATH OF NEDA AGHA SOLTAN

This section presents an analysis of the case of Neda Agha Soltan from a dramatic diffusion perspective and with a focus on adaptation. The methodology and approach is described in the first subsection. The analysis is presented in three following subsections: the first provides a factual background; the second outlines core elements in Iran's political-cultural schema; and the third provides an extended analysis of the formation of the Neda injustice symbol.

## A NOTE ON METHODOLOGY AND APPROACH

Methodologically, the analysis makes use of a broad selection of empirical data sources. Given the theoretical focus on resonance and critical engagement, attention is primarily on the way Neda's death has been discursively infused with meaning by non-Iranian actors: echoing the definition of global social movements introduced in chapter 1, these include, primarily, media, activists, networked citizens, and politicians. Media sources play a central role and are used in a dual manner: on the one hand, media, as noted, were among the main actors in the formation of the Neda injustice symbol, on the other hand, journalistic work serves as a crucial source for factual information about Neda, her life, and the circumstances of her death. Two documentaries by HBO and BBC exemplify this dual role. On the one hand, the documentaries uncover relevant information about Neda and her death. On the other, they are also study objects in their own right as they are actively engaged in the construction of the Neda injustice symbol and its associated meanings. Meaning infusion is analyzed against *Iran's political-cultural schema*. Since this schema is at least partly constituted by the actions of Iranian authorities, their interventions in the aftermath of Neda's death constitute a crucial element in parts of the analysis. The analysis mainly focuses on approximately the first six months following Neda's death on June 20, 2009. In the last part of the chapter, however, observations are made regarding Neda's stability as an injustice symbol. This includes a focus on cultural products and presence on YouTube.

## BACKGROUND

Neda did not have a history as an activist, but took part in the postelection protests as a morally outraged citizen (BBC, 2009; HBO, 2010). The June 20 protests had been preceded by several days of protests but were widely perceived to be the most dangerous since the elections. In his Friday-prayer remarks the day before, supreme leader Ayatollah

Ali Khamenei had thus issued a stern warning that protesters would face potential consequences if demonstrations persisted (BBC, 2009). During the protests on June 20, her music teacher, Hamid Panahi, accompanied Neda. The two were heading back to their car when Neda was hit by a gunshot and fell to the ground. A 48-seconds-long cell phone video recorded by a bystander shows the collapsed Neda being attended to by her music teacher and a doctor, Arash Hejazi, a fellow protestor and, later, a key witness and source in journalistic accounts of the event. In the chaotic and low-quality footage Panahi is heard screaming "Neda, stay with me." A few minutes later Neda dies at the scene (Assmann and Assmann, 2010). Fellow protestors immediately identified a Basij militiaman as the shooter and dragged him from his motorcycle. In the chaos of the event, he was eventually released by the crowd (BBC, 2009; HBO, 2010) (no charges have ever been pressed by authorities against him or any other individual).[3] The (apparent) identification of the shooter immediately established a clear link between the Iranian regime and Neda's death. The 48-seconds video was uploaded to YouTube and Facebook by an Iranian asylum seeker in Holland who was contacted by a friend in Iran who had accidentally recorded Neda's death (Tait and Weaver, 2009) and had inadvertently become a citizen journalist (Andén-Papadopoulos, 2014; Mortensen, 2011). Another, shorter video recorded by an anonymous person zoomed in on Neda's face and showed profuse bleeding from her nose and mouth covering her face. Within hours the videos were circulating the globe via YouTube, Facebook, and Twitter (Assmann and Assmann, 2010). From the social networks, they rapidly made their way into the mainstream media (Mortensen, 2011: 7). The Neda story was only shortly confined to the networks of global communication. Soon people and organizations all over the world took to the streets with images of Neda and messages such as "We Are All Neda" and "I Am Neda."

## IRAN'S POLITICAL-CULTURAL SCHEMA

The dominant political-cultural schema available for Neda's death has deep roots in recent global history and the continuing conflict between Iran and the West since the Iranian Revolution in 1979. What follows is obviously a simplification in that it condenses almost 35 years of history into a few paragraphs. The goal here is thus not to offer a full account of the relationship between Iran and the West but to point to some of the defining moments in that history and to outline the major political and cultural themes in this conflict. Since the 1979 ousting of Shah Mohammad Reza Pahlavi in the Iranian Revolution led by Ayatollah Ruhollah Khomeini, Iran has been a consistent target for activists, politicians, and states in the West. The enmity between Iran and, especially, the United States came into full global view already around the time of the Iranian Islamic Revolution. In November 1979, a group associated with and backed by the new regime, took 52 Americans hostage inside the American embassy (the hostage crisis ended with a negotiated release after 444 days) (Houghton, 2001). The crisis was a major global news story until the release of the hostages. In a famous speech in late 1979 that set the tone for the fractious relationship and acquired significant global resonance, Khomeini thus referred to the United States as "the great Satan"—a label empirically founded mainly in the United States' long-standing support for Israel and for the Iranian monarchy under Shah Pahlavi (1941–1979). In 1989, the relationship between Iran and the West came under new strain when Ayatollah Khomeini issued a fatwa (a legal judgment made by a senior Muslim cleric) for Salman Rushdie's novel, *The Satanic Verses* (published in 1988). The fatwa explicitly called for Rushdie to be killed for blasphemy. The fatwa was followed by protests and attacks in several countries around the world (including in the West) and led to severing of diplomatic ties between Iran and number of Western countries (Pipes, 2003). The fatwa has been reaffirmed on several occasions since Khomeini's death in 1989 and even in recent years (Tait, 2012). During the last few decades, the relationship between Iran and the West has been dominated by the issue of nuclear power and weapons. A string of reports from the International Atomic Energy Agency (IAEA) purports to document that Iran is progressing toward the development of nuclear weapons. The issue of nuclear energy and

weapons remains an obstacle for the normalization of political relations between Iran and the West (Baghat, 2006). Another thorny
issue, exacerbated since 9/11, has been Iran's continued support
for organizations considered by the West to be terrorist organizations (Baghat, 2003; Byman, 2008) and its related anti-Semitism
(expressed, inter alia, in President Mahmoud Ahmadinejad's highly
publicized and widely criticized denials of the Holocaust). The combination of nuclear politics and terrorist support famously led US
president George W. Bush, in his 2002 State of the Union address, to
locate Iran within a global "axis of evil." While these incidents and
problems are clearly related to international relations, Iran has also
been a repeated focal point for human rights activists. For several
decades, reports from Amnesty International (2013) and Human
Rights Watch (2013b) have pointed to consistent and serious human
rights violations in Iran. A significant element in this criticism per-
tains to women's rights and repression under Islamic law.

## SYMBOL FORMATION

The political-cultural schema globally available for Iran thus builds
on a number of binaries and major themes that cast Iran as representing everything that we in the West are not: religious-secular; oppres-
sion/control-freedom; democratic-nondemocratic; rational-irrational,
and so on. The themes are clearly linked. For example, the religious
basis of Iranian politics and society is viewed as incompatible with
democracy and women's rights in a Western conception. The guiding
argument to be pursued in the following is that the formation of the
Neda global injustice symbol has drawn significantly from elements
in this overall political-cultural schema. This is identified at four
different levels: in the attempts to place Neda in a global history of
struggles for freedom and democracy; in the Iranian regime's attempt
to de-symbolize her; in the infusion of certain character traits; and in
the visual and emotional drama of her death. In the last part of the
analysis the angle shifts slightly toward a discussion of the stability
and continued resonance of the Neda injustice symbol after the formative period in 2009.

*From National to Global History*

The videos of Neda's death almost instantly drew reactions from the highest political level. This was especially the case in the United States where, for historical reasons outlined above (and also reflecting a politically vociferous Iranian community in the United States), Iran has consistently played a central role in foreign policy. In a June 23 press conference, President Barack Obama famously referred to the videos as "heartbreaking," going on to say that "anybody who sees it knows that there's something fundamentally unjust about that." While Obama's remarks did not clearly confer specific meanings and values on Neda, such infusion was made strongly on the same day from the Senate floor by an emotional John McCain (R-Arizona) (2009):

> So, Mr. President, a debate has been going on as to how much the United States of America...should speak out in favor, and support, of these brave Iranians...in their quest for the fundamentals of freedom and democracy that we have enjoyed for more than a couple of centuries.

In the speech, McCain linked these general observations directly to the case of Neda: "So, Mr. President, today, I and all America, pay tribute to a brave young woman who was trying to exercise her fundamental human rights and was killed on the streets of Tehran." In the speech McCain anchored the protests in Iran in general and Neda's death in particular in a predominantly Western historical experience of struggling for and obtaining democratic and human rights. Despite the fact that little was known about Neda and her background at this point in time, McCain unequivocally interpreted her death as an individual sacrifice in the larger historic struggle for democracy—a global struggle in which Iran is evidently on the wrong side (and the West, of course, on the right side). The sacrificial theme was invoked in several early media accounts and postings on social media in which Neda was referred to as Iran's Joan of Arc (e.g., Putz, 2009; this interpretation is repeated in McCain's speech).[4] It was also, with some delay, confirmed by people close to Neda. According to Caspian Makan (Neda's boyfriend), when he tried to persuade her to stay away from the street protests as they got increasingly violent, she responded by saying, "If I get shot in the heart or arrested, it's not important because we are all responsible for our future" (quoted in Athanasiadis, 2009). Neda, as a result, is portrayed as a fearless woman ready to sacrifice her life for the greater cause of freedom and democracy. This portrayal disembeds her from national history and places her in a global history of people or icons who have sacrificed or risked their life for the common and collective good of freedom and democracy (e.g., Gandhi, Luther King, Mandela, and Suu Kyi; see also chapter 2). Only after this disembedding exercise could she be returned, as it were, to the Iranian context, now equipped with new meanings accessible and intelligible for a Western audience.

The overall thrust and consequence of these interpretations was in a sense to erase the accidental nature of Neda's death (this reached a climax in the 2012 short film, *I am Neda*, in which her death is overloaded with almost prophetic meaning; see also the subsection "Stability and Continued Resonance" below). The killing of Neda appears to have been random or even accidental for two reasons. First, there is no evident reason that we know of why Neda should have been singled out by the shooter from the large number of demonstrators (some, however, link her death to her beauty and the fact that Iranian militia and security forces tend to single out beautiful women for aggression; see HBO, 2010; see also discussions in the subsection "Character and Visuals"). Second, and in continuation of the above point, Neda was not at the forefront of protest but participated mainly as one concerned individual among many. This is not to say that she was in the street on June 20 out of curiosity or by chance. Accounts suggest that she had been to several protest events since the elections on June 12 (BBC, 2009), actively participating and shouting (HBO, 2010; her behavior in this regard is described by Arash Hejazi, the doctor and protestor present when she died), and that she harbored deep grievances about the Iranian regime. Yet, it is quite evident that she did not belong to the organizational core of protesters but acted mainly on an individual basis.[5] It might, of course, be said that the degree of injustice is not dependent on whether the death was accidental or premeditated. This is only partly true, however. As noted in the

"Dramatic Cross-Border Diffusion" section and in chapter 1, it is not the injustice of a violent person-event that turns it into an injustice symbol. The injustice must be seen to represent a wider problematic (that is linkable to existing injustice frames). Such a link would have been easier to establish if Neda had verifiably been a leading protester. Had that been the case, it could have been claimed that she was killed in precisely that capacity. In the absence of such an anchor, adopters were required to engage more actively in meaning infusion to provide her death with symbolic and thus universalizing potential.

*De-symbolization*

Paradoxically, the Iranian regime itself contributed strongly to the formation of the Neda injustice symbol. Paradoxically, because it could have played the "bad apple" card and claimed the shooting to have been an accident. As shown at the end of the preceding subsection such an account would have had some empirical credibility. Had the regime employed a combination of taking *general* responsibility for the event and *individualizing* the immediate cause of her death (i.e., identifying and penalizing the shooter), it could potentially have taken at least some of the political air out of the emotionally and morally charged attempts to link Neda's death with struggles for freedom and democracy. The power of such a strategy would have resided in its ability to disturb Iran's political-cultural schema. As noted in the "Dramatic Cross-Border Diffusion" section and in chapter 1, states and other perpetrators of violence considered unjust by others, often engage in *de-symbolization*. Only few days after Neda's death, on June 26, in the Friday sermon, the leading Iranian cleric Ayatollah Ahmed Khatami accused the protesters of staging Neda's death: "The proof and evidence shows that they have done it themselves and have raised propaganda against the system" (quoted in Gorman, 2009). And on June 25, the Iranian ambassador to Mexico, Mohammad Hassan Ghadiri, in an interview with Wolf Blitzer of the CNN, pointed to possible CIA involvement: "If the CIA wants to kill some people and attribute that to the elements of the government, and then choosing a girl, would be something good for them because it would have much higher impact" (quoted in Malcolm, 2009). Later, in a CNN interview with Larry

King on September 25, Iranian president Mahmoud Ahmadinejad took denial to the highest political level, suggesting that the incident had been fabricated to cast a negative global light on the regime (CNN, 2009). And in January 2010, Iranian state television broadcast a documentary claiming that "forensic evidence and statements by security officials show Neda was not killed in the way shown by Western media. Neda was in fact killed after playing the role in a plot whose fake pictures were shown over and over again" (quoted in Mackey, 2010). These blatant attempts at deflecting accusations, disregarding facts, and displacing guilt only served to strengthen the formation of the Neda global injustice symbol. It did so because it exposed and reaffirmed central themes in the Iranian schema. In particular it tapped into the rational-irrational theme empirically anchored, inter alia, in President Ahmadinejad's public denials of the Holocaust. The paradoxical effect was that by trying to avoid blame, the regime seemed to only confirm and even widen the moral distance between itself and Neda. This is a reverse proportional dynamic in which the victim's innocence and purity increases as the direct or indirect perpetrator's moral position decreases (see Olesen, 2013b, for a related point in the context of the Egyptian Revolution in 2011). The moral-political corruption of the Iranian regime was further strengthened as it appeared how Neda's family had been pressured by authorities not to mourn her publicly and denied a traditional funeral service (HBO, 2010; Naghibi, 2011: 65).[6]

*Character and Visuals*
As already briefly shown, personal character traits (some of them powerfully supported by photographs) have played a central role in the formation of the Neda injustice symbol. A key element in this process has been a kind of political depoliticization of Neda. What this seemingly self-contradictory term suggests is how, in most accounts, Neda was not associated with any specific ideological or party political affiliation but cast as an individual striving for freedom and democracy in a relatively generalized sense. In a 2010 HBO documentary directed by Antony Thomas, Neda's family thus describes her as a rebel since her early years. As a youth and grown woman,

they recount, she felt uncomfortable submitting to the standards of behavior and appearance set by the religious authorities. The image of Neda that transpires is that of an innocent and delicate bird in a cage (a portrait underlined by the repeatedly reported fact that one of Neda's main passions was traveling): "Neda, outspoken, brave, clashing with authority almost from the start, a free spirit confined by a regime that does not value these qualities in a woman" (HBO, 2010: 1:45–2.00). In the last part of the voiceover, Neda's life and death is clearly associated with the struggle for women's rights in Islamic Iran (according to Naghibi, 2011: 64, this line of interpretation was also dominant among diasporic Iranians in the United States). As argued earlier, the issue of women's rights is a core element in the oppression/control-freedom and religious-secular themes in the Iranian schema. The point here is obviously not to deny the relevance of this issue. Rather, what is notable is how Neda's death and its immediate context did not have a women's rights dimension per se. The demonstrations where she died were, as already mentioned, motivated by the fraudulent presidential election in Iran on June 12 and, in a wider sense, by a general dissatisfaction with the regime in broad circles of the Iranian population—not women's rights as such. While certain observations pertaining to Neda's life definitely warrant a women's rights angle, the very direct link created in the aftermath is clearly, to some extent at least, a projection anchored in Iran's political-cultural schema.

The image of a determined and rebellious woman is contrasted with the description of Neda as a joyful, positive, pure, and almost ephemeral person. In an early and widely circulated quote, Hamid Panahi called her "a person full of joy" and "a beam of light" (quoted in Borzou, 2009). And according to her sister, she never stopped smiling (HBO, 2010). This combination of determination and kindness, of strength and frailty, is a central character trait in several of the global icons referred to earlier (e.g., Mandela and Suu Kyi; see chapter 2). In the case of Neda, such accounts were lent powerful visual support by the set of pre-death images circulated after June 20. Two of the best-known images show Neda looking directly at us, smiling beautifully: one of them with her hand under her cheek and the other with her head slightly bowed to one side. In these images she is in a sense universalized; she could be a citizen of any country (Naghibi, 2011: 66) (Neda's universality is also underlined by references to her aforementioned passion for traveling; and in the HBO documentary we are told how her book collection was globally oriented with Persian language copies of Emily Bronte's *Wuthering Heights* and Herman Hesse's *Siddhartha*).[7]

Neda's young, vibrant, beautiful, smiling face furthermore offered a powerful contrast to the visual dimension of Iran's political-cultural schema. Visually, this schema is associated with veiled women and the serious looking and bearded faces of Iran's male-only politicians and clerics. Neda's beauty attained an additional layer of meaning through the above-mentioned allegations that she was targeted precisely because of her beauty and un-Islamic appearance. There is no hard evidence supporting this interpretation in the case of Neda. Yet, the claim makes intuitive sense because beauty can be readily contrasted with the attempt to control women's bodies and appearances in Iran. Beauty, within this political-cultural schema, thus acquired a potentially political meaning. The photographs of Neda not only contrasted with certain dominant themes in the Iranian schema but also, in a simpler and emotional manner, with the images of her death. What is particularly powerful about the June 20 videos is their extreme intimacy, zooming in on Neda's face as blood streams out from her mouth and nose, creating a chaotic pattern across her face. The emotional and moral distance between the smiling Neda and the dying Neda is immense and unbearable and constitutes a moral shock for the viewer (see Olesen, 2013b, for a related observation in relation to the case of Khaled Said in Egypt).

*Stability and Continued Resonance*

The analysis above has focused primarily on the period immediately following Neda's death in 2009. As noted in chapter 1, and in chapter 2 on Nelson Mandela, the symbolic process may be considered to have various phases. While Neda thus achieved more or less instantaneous symbolic status during her dramatic diffusion in the summer of 2009 and approximately the next six months, it is of central interest to consider the extent to which she keeps resonating and the forms in which her symbolic status has been preserved. As is the case with many violent person-events transformed into injustice symbols, the date of death/violence (and sometimes birthdays) are seized as opportunities for expressions of sorrow and protest (in this sense such moments are akin to the process of moral-political remembering analyzed in chapter 4 on Rwanda). For example, on the fourth anniversary of Neda's death (June 20, 2013), images of Neda's mother, Hajar Rostami Motlagh, grieving at her grave in Iran, were circulated on YouTube.[8] Hajar Rostami Motlagh also gave interviews to the International Campaign for Human Rights in Iran (2013), lamenting and criticizing the lack of legal justice in Neda's case (as mentioned earlier, no one has ever been convicted of the crime). Obviously, these activities do not have the degree of intensity and attention as those of 2009 but they do indicate that Neda has achieved a permanent presence in global society. This presence or stability is also evident in the cultural productions that now surround the Neda symbol (see also "Dramatizing the Rwandan Genocide" subsection in chapter 4). In the wake of Neda's death, a small industry of political merchandise such as t-shirts, posters, and coffee cups emerged. While these are relatively time-bound products, Neda also became the object of more lasting cultural expressions such as a series of sculptures created by American artist Paula Slater (Naghibi, 2011; Stage, 2011). And in 2012, an award winning short film, *I Am Neda*, was published, which gave an account of Neda's life up to and during the events on June 20, 2009. Parallel with these professional cultural products, numerous amateur political and cultural productions paying tribute to Neda are available on YouTube.[9] Continuing the discussion on global moral memories in chapter 4, we may thus think of YouTube as a kind of global memory archive that ensures a stable global presence and visibility for symbols and icons and that furthermore becomes a site for their continuous symbol formation (as evidenced by the fact that several tribute videos have been created and posted in 2012 and 2013).

## CONCLUSION

Through the graphic and immediately circulated images of her death, Neda reached the global public sphere in a more or less unfiltered, sudden, and raw form. The analysis demonstrates how this "material" was transformed into a global injustice symbol through a globally available Iranian political-cultural schema. The Iranian schema is constituted by a number of dichotomous core themes: religious-secular; oppression/control-freedom; democratic-nondemocratic; rational-irrational. The operation of the themes is visible on at least four levels: first, Neda and her death was placed in a wider historic and global struggle for democracy and human rights in which Iran was cast as a negative other; second, the themes in the schema were confirmed, as it were, by the Iranian regime itself as it denied any responsibility for Neda's death and even tried to blame it on non-Iranian actors such as the CIA and Western journalists; third, certain character traits and previous behavior were highlighted to portray Neda as innocent and as a victim of Islamic Iran (this involved emphasizing her relevance for women's rights); fourth, these traits were supported by the circulation of pre-death photographs (showing a beautiful, young, smiling Neda) that provided a contrast to the visual dimension of the Iranian schema (male, old, somber, dark). In sum, the symbolic interaction between Neda and the Iranian schema gave her an *ideological and visual accessibility* that significantly facilitated global resonance.

Meaning adaptation can be viewed from various angles. On the one hand, it is evident that the formation of injustice symbols like Neda reflects dominant ideational structures at a global level. What is claimed here is obviously not that the Neda symbol was manufactured and manipulated (i.e., not anchored in observable facts). Rather, some of these facts have been *amplified* because they resonated particularly well with core themes in the existing Iranian political-cultural schema. This is the essence of *meaning adaptation*. On the other hand, the very formation of the Neda injustice symbol potentially impacts the Iranian schema. As noted in the "Dramatic Cross-Border Diffusion" section, schemas are not static but constantly modified through, in particular, new empirical events. It could thus be argued that the Neda event has disturbed and perhaps relaxed the Iranian schema. Neda, and the Green Movement protests in 2009, have added a new dimension to the image of a secure and monolithic regime and a more or less subdued civil society. The 2009 protests, which were symbolized and given permanent global status through Neda's death, demonstrated that protest and activism occur even under extremely closed political opportunities. As such, the Neda symbol has facilitated an image of Iran that is more complex than the dominant Iranian political-cultural schema allows for. A similar pattern may be found in relation to Malala Yousafzai (see chapter 1) who has also been strongly interpreted through a Western-based political-cultural schema that understands Pakistan and other Muslim countries to be underdeveloped in relation to women's and girls' right to, for example, education. While this schema is empirically grounded in conditions in certain parts of the Muslim world, it also implicitly celebrates who "we" are and the historical progress that we have created and define ourselves in relation to. Yet in a way related to the observations on Neda, the Malala case and symbol also serves as a window into political processes and movements often lost in media accounts—a window that shows us *complex* societies engaged in political and cultural struggles.

The argument advanced in the chapter is not that dramatic cross-border diffusion of violent person-events is a new phenomenon as such. The struggle against Apartheid, for example, produced several well-known individual injustice symbols such as Steven Biko, a South African antiapartheid activist killed in police custody in 1977, and Hector Pieterson, a young student killed during the Soweto uprising in 1976. Yet, taking up a thread laid out earlier, the formation and circulation of injustice symbols and other kinds of memes are significantly facilitated in the contemporary era by two types of media technology: portable devices with visual documentation functions (i.e., smartphones and tablets) and social media that enable rapid dissemination via vast interpersonal networks. As a concluding comment, it might be argued that at a philosophical/critical level the formation of individual injustice symbols is problematic. The fact that global attention is nurtured by dramatic and often visually powerful instances of violence against individuals inadvertently points to the many (daily) injustices that do not gain attention in the same way. It demonstrates how global attention to suffering and injustice is often emotionally rather than philosophically and politically driven and, as a result, unsystematic and unequal. For example, exiled Iranian journalist Masih Alinejad has created a project focused on giving voice and attention to some of the lesser-known activists killed during the protests in 2009 (Deghan, 2013) (this theme is revisited in the concluding chapter 6).

# A GLOBAL SOCIETY?

CHAPTER 1 ARGUED THAT THE STUDY OF GLOBAL INJUSTICE SYMBOLS and global social movements is sociologically important because it enables an empirically grounded discussion of *global society*. This reflects the Durkheimian foundation of the book, which indicates that the analysis of symbols is, fundamentally, an analysis of *society*. Symbols and society are closely connected because the former are carriers of collectively held values and meanings about right and wrong, good and bad, desirable and undesirable. As such symbols are, at least potentially, highly political. In a dialectical fashion symbols are both the *outcome* of politics and ideational resources employed *in* politics. This understanding has been a focal point in all the preceding case studies. It has been a guiding assumption of the book that it is possible to study symbolic processes not only at the local and national level, which were Durkheim's analytical levels, but at the global level as well. Hopefully, the case studies have convincingly demonstrated the feasibility and usefulness of such an approach. Of course, we cannot simply infer from the book's cases that a global society exists. The concluding section of each of the case chapters thus emphasizes a number of themes that motivate critique and problematization. This chapter attempts to balance the various threads laid out in the book in order to assess the *realities* and *limitations* of global society. It begins with a discussion of the realities of global society, that is, observations supporting the existence of a global society. It then moves on to a critical discussion of its limitations and, especially, the power relationships, biases, and political conflicts that traverse it. The purpose of these discussions is to summarize the key analytical points and findings of the four case studies and to form the basis of a discussion, elaboration, and critique of Alexander's (2007, 2012) concept of the *global civil sphere*, which, as noted in chapter 1, is intimately connected to that of global society. The chapter concludes by outlining the lessons that the book has to offer for the field of global social movement studies.

## THE REALITIES OF GLOBAL SOCIETY

All the case studies provide evidence of a global society in different ways. They also demonstrate that global social movements are a driving force in it. This observation may be broken down into four themes that also reflect the case studies in the book.

### COLLECTIVE ICONS

Chapter 2, on Nelson Mandela, discussed and showed how Mandela the person has been transformed into a global *political icon* and, thus, a carrier of political values concerning democracy, human rights, solidarity, and reconciliation. Mandela's iconic transformation covered several decades and was initiated already before he disappeared from public life in 1964 following the so-called Rivonia trial. The process gathered pace in the late 1970s in relation to Mandela's sixtieth birthday and climaxed in the late 1980s and early 1990s. After the climaxing period, Mandela has not attracted the same level of attention but has become firmly established as a global political icon, as evidenced, for example, in the numerous biographies published in the period after his release. The more or less unanimous praise that followed his death on December 5, 2013, and the globally televised and emotional occasion of his funeral significantly testifies to his genuinely global status as a kind of democratic and human rights totem. Mandela's globality and iconicity is intimately connected with the *global social movement* (widely referred to as the global antiapartheid movement) that elevated him to the global stage. This process, as noted above, climaxed with the birthday celebration at Wembley in 1988 and, only two years later in the same place, a show celebrating Mandela's release from prison. Mandela, in other words, does not only have a central position *in* global society but he is also its creation in the sense that his iconicity was forged through the action of a global social movement actively inscribing on him certain political values. The icon is thus closely tied to and perhaps even integrated with its creators. While the iconic process was founded in the empirical *biography* of Mandela, this biography and its "materials" were made visible and amplified by *agents* with an interest in iconizing Mandela. The resonance of these activities in turn depended strongly on Mandela's fit with *audience* expectations and dominant global ideals. The climax event at Wembley in 1990 was consequently not only a celebration of Mandela and the ANC but also to some extent a celebration of the global society (represented in the global antiapartheid movement) that had played a significant part in his release from prison and in the collapse of apartheid. Mandela is part of a wider *symbolic family* that includes antiapartheid (and globally visible and resonant) related places and events such as, for example, Robben Island (where Mandela was incarcerated), the Sharpeville massacre in 1962, and the Soweto uprising in 1976. The global political iconography perspective is expandable to other cases. Chapters 1 and 2, for example, mention global icons such as Aung San Suu Kyi, Dalai Lama, Malala Yousafzai, Martin Luther King, and Mohandas Gandhi. These are all, in different ways and contexts, globally resonant carriers of values of democracy and human rights.

## Collective Grievances

The chapter on Guantanamo Bay analyzed how *grievance communities* are, at least partly, constituted through shared injustice symbols. A grievance community is an ideological and identity based network of individuals and organizations loosely connected via collective perceptions of injustice. Grievance communities are not exclusive to the global level. Yet, it was argued that injustice symbols play an especially important role for *global* grievance communities since these are imagined and mediated communities of individuals and organizations scattered over the world. Globally visible and resonant injustice symbols serve to provide common points of reference in such loose networks of limited physical and spatial copresence. The global grievance community underlying the symbolization of Guantanamo Bay is rooted in *political Islam*. Within this political-cultural schema, Guantanamo Bay symbolizes, at one level, what is wrong with the current war on terror and, at a deeper level, the historically anchored aggression of the West toward the Muslim parts of the world. As such, Guantanamo is part of a wider *injustice hierarchy*. Guantanamo functions as an injustice symbol for a wide variety of actors. This chapter focuses on its role in radical Islamist terrorism and especially in the activities of al-Qaeda, which actively employs Guantanamo to highlight and expose the moral corruption of, in particular, the United States. It is furthermore utilized in discursive legitimations of political violence directed toward the United States and is consequently a concern for political authorities and security analysts working on terror and political violence prevention. Guantanamo is part of a *symbolic family* including, for example, the Danish Muhammad cartoons, the Abu Ghraib photographs, and Palestine. Political Islam is today a genuinely global phenomenon. The analytical and theoretical purchase of speaking of political Islam as a grievance community is that it strikes a middle ground between viewing it either as a more or less united ideology or as a phenomenon with limited internal coherence. Grievance communities have social movement elements and potentials, but the two concepts cannot be collapsed. Much of the specific political activity over the symbolization of Guantanamo Bay has the character of a global social movement consisting of various actors, including al-Qaeda. What is interesting when compared, for example, with the global antiapartheid movement is how the movement surrounding Guantanamo Bay may be globally dispersed but operates with a non-global worldview whose proposed solutions are based on a sharp distinction between Muslims and non-Muslims (the moral-political value base of the antiapartheid movement was premised on the idea of human equality across geographic, religious, and political differences). The concept of grievance communities can be applied to other phenomena. Extreme Right actors and sympathizers, for example, may be grounded in a national and exclusive worldview,

but in ways similar with political Islam it is a globally dispersed grievance community indirectly connected through shared perceptions of
injustice and with its own symbolic vocabulary.

## COLLECTIVE MEMORIES

In chapter 4 the case was made that the Rwandan genocide has become
a globally shared *moral memory*. The moral memory of the Rwandan
genocide concerns not only the victims and causes of the genocide
but also to a significant extent those third parties, mainly states and
international institutions, who observed the horrors without adequate
intervention. The Rwandan genocide is consequently remembered as
a *shameful* event for global society. Injustice symbols, following the
Durkheimian theoretical thread of the book, are value carriers that
contain ideas not only about who we want to be but, equally, about
whom we do *not* want to be. These two value sets are obviously closely
interconnected. The Rwandan genocide thus sparked a global moral-
political soul searching to express guilt and regret over what had *not*
been done as well as to set up procedures to avoid similar events in
the future. While memories always concern what happened in the
past, *moral-political* memories are distinct in containing *three temporalities* in which the past guides the present and motivates future-ori-
ented institutional and organizational initiatives and arrangements.
As shown by Durkheim and other sociologists and anthropologists,
memories are essential not only in the constitution of individual life
narratives but also, at a collective level, for the historical and moral-
political coherence of society. The activities surrounding the political
moralization of the Rwandan memory should be conceived of as a
global social movement. While states and international institutions
played a leading role in the formation of the Rwandan memory, the
process was much broader than this and included, most notably,
activist organizations and media acting in a moral-political capacity.
The moral-political memory process related to the Rwandan genocide
consisted of four elements: institutionalization (making the Rwandan
genocide an object for international legal prosecution); regret (states'
expressions of guilt over nonintervention); evocation (the employment

of the Rwandan genocide in relation to contemporary events such as the Darfur crisis); and dramatization (the use and treatment of the genocide in cultural productions such as books and movies). The concept of global moral memories is applicable to other cases and in fact has a sometimes-blurred boundary in relation to some of the other cases and concepts discussed in the book. All injustice symbols, as they recede in time, become injustice memories. What distinguishes the moral-political memory category to which the Rwandan genocide belongs is that the memorizing collective feels some kind of guilt, either regarding the onset of some atrocity or the failure to act when it was occurring. For example, while the death of Neda Agha Soltan, discussed in chapter 5, may eventually become an injustice memory, it does not contain the element of guilt and regret that the Rwandan genocide and other comparable events do. Within this category, to which the concept of moral memories is primarily applicable, we find, for example, the Holocaust and the ethnic cleansing processes during the Balkan Wars, most powerfully symbolized by the Srebrenica massacre in the 1990s. These events, like the Rwandan genocide, remain lingering wounds in global collective memory and keep informing politics today.

## COLLECTIVE IMAGES

The chapter on Neda Agha Soltan emphasized, among other things, the power and role of images in global processes of *dramatic diffusion*. In 2009, Neda was shot and killed during protests against fraudulent elections in Iran. Bystander and cell phone recorded images of the dying Neda went globally viral shortly after they were recorded. Globally circulated images often involve *violent person-events*, that is, events where individuals are subjected to undeserved violence directly or indirectly related to and committed by *systems of authority*. Images are globally resonant partly because of their ability to invoke emotional responses and *moral shocks* in the viewing audience. The photographic documentation of unjust violence (or the results of it) seems to elicit universal reactions of sorrow, anger, and frustration. The rapid and network based diffusion of the images and the immediate reactions of condemnation and moral shock constituted a global social movement. The concern with distant and suffering others is a compelling expression of a globality in which people and places are morally and politically interconnected. Images such as those of Neda Agha Soltan become part of our shared collective imagination. In this sense images have some affinity with moral memories. Images in other words are central to the way we collectively and globally remember certain events: the Holocaust and the Balkan Wars, for example, both have a well-defined and globally well-known visual dimension. And the Vietnam War is to a significant extent also remembered through iconic images such as those from My Lai and Nick Ut's photographs of children fleeing from a napalm attack. Images have played a moral and political role since the invention of photography. However, there are reasons to argue that their significance is increasing in the new media and communication environment that has been emerging in recent decades. Portable recording devices carried by individuals increase the potential for *citizen journalism*, while the digitalized nature of such recordings and the proliferation of circuits for their circulation mean that information can reach enormous audiences in very little time. Web-based technologies and platforms further provide new opportunities for the preservation of images in global collective memory. YouTube and Wikipedia today serve as a kind of *global archives* that ensure stable and constant global visibility and availability of iconic images of injustice. The mentioning of images from the Holocaust, the Balkan Wars, and the Vietnam War indicates that the study of dramatic visual diffusion can be adapted to a number of other cases and not only to the present. In the present situation, examples abound. In one, which also connects to chapter 3 on grievance communities, the publication in 2004 of photographs of prisoner abuse at the prison facility at Abu Ghraib generated moral shocks globally (although this interpretation was contested by some). The Abu Ghraib photos are now perhaps the best-known visual representation of the dark side of the war against terror.

## THE LIMITATIONS OF GLOBAL SOCIETY

The preceding section offered evidence of the realities of global society. The analyses, however, also point to limitations, conflicts, power relations, and biases. These are addressed under five rubrics that draw their material from across the cases.

### IDOLIZATION AND SIMPLIFICATION

As shown in chapter 2 on Nelson Mandela, political icons are value carriers. They are, in other words, socialized and universalized individuals. Yet the process of iconic formation also involves some degree of *idolization* and, consequently, *reduction* and *simplification*. Reduction occurs when a wider social, political, and cultural problematic is condensed in such a way that they come to be *represented* by certain people, images, or events. This in many ways echoes the definition of symbols proposed in chapter 1, where it was argued how symbols are able to encapsulate complex situations in recognizable and often emotionally compelling forms. However, these strengths also contain a number of inherent problems. First, iconization may stand in the way of deeper knowledge of an underlying condition. For example, in its most popular phase in the 1980s, antiapartheid more or less became a question of freeing Mandela, the implicit assumption being that with Mandela's freedom everything would be put in its right place. One could engage therefore with antiapartheid without much knowledge of the complexities of South African society and the challenges awaiting it after the collapse of apartheid. However, there is little doubt that such idolization and simplification was the very foundation of the extremely *popular* appeal of the antiapartheid struggle. And as shown in chapter 2, iconization was in fact a strategy endorsed and pursued by key actors in the antiapartheid movement. Iconization, in other words, is a double-edged sword where popular appeal (and with that potentially increased political pressure on targets) comes at the price of some degree of simplification. Second, as noted above, iconization is often part of a conscious and strategic choice. This implies that the person chosen for iconic status may be one among several potential candidates. As such it is a choice with political implications. When

Mandela became the face of antiapartheid, it thus included an implicit or explicit favorization of the ANC over other South African organizations and movements involved in the struggle against apartheid (e.g., the Black Consciousness Movement and the Inkatha Freedom Party). This point is closely related to that above, as these complexities and diversities are often lost in the iconic process. Global iconization may therefore, at least potentially, generate conflicts locally and nationally when the iconic status awarded at the global level is not recognized or is challenged by political actors at the local and national level. Third, and in a point related somewhat to the theme of *amnesia* below, iconization potentially erases or hides history. Condensing the antiapartheid struggle in the figure of Mandela tends to cloud the fact that the dissolution of apartheid came via the suffering and sacrifice of thousands of individuals whose fates and achievements do not have nearly the same status as that of Mandela. This observation, however, is valid mainly at a global level. At the local and national level, we may thus encounter local and national icons whose meanings offer either counter-narratives or supplements to the globalized icon.

### DIVISION AND CONTESTATION

While some global injustice symbols have a global unifying capacity others are arguably more divisive. Guantanamo Bay, it was argued earlier, is a symbolic center in a globally constituted grievance community anchored in the political-cultural schema of political Islam. However, it was also noted that the globality of this community is a reduced one in the sense that it is premised on a sharp *dividing* line separating Muslims and non-Muslims. Guantanamo Bay is consequently employed in the political communication of, for example, al-Qaeda to expose a deep political and cultural rift in global society that cannot and should not be mended. Other injustice symbols employed by political Islamists (e.g., the Muhammad cartoons) serve a related purpose. The focus on the dividing and *conflictive* character of global injustice symbols is condensed here under two themes. First, Guantanamo Bay is not only employed as an injustice symbol from within the schema of political Islam. For many individuals, activists, and politicians concerned with the negative democratic and human rights consequences of the war on terror, the prison at Guantanamo Bay has been a target since its inception. While, say, al-Qaeda and Human Rights Watch, may both find Guantanamo Bay problematic, they do so from within different and in some regards opposing political-cultural schemas. As such the study of global injustice symbols is also the study of how global society and the global public sphere, which constitutes its communicative framework (see chapter 1), are characterized by *competing* political-cultural schemas that may potentially impute the same symbols with different meanings. Second, what is notable about such dividing and conflictive symbols is how they often produce one another in a *dialectical spiral.* The injustice symbol of Palestine, for example, was a major motivation in the formation of al-Qaeda. When this organization attacked the World Trade Center on September 11, 2001, it created a powerful injustice symbol for most people in the United States and elsewhere. This attack in turn set in motion a global war on terror, which in itself has produced a number of powerful global injustice symbols, including Guantanamo Bay and the Abu Ghraib photos.

## AMNESIA AND ERASURE

Some of the most powerful injustice symbols are also *moral memories.* Moral memories involve collective reflections on what society should and should not be. Yet moral remembering is also, at least potentially, moral *forgetting* or *amnesia.* In chapter 4 on the Rwandan genocide, the moral remembering primarily concerned the lack of attention and intervention on the part of those non-Rwandan actors and audiences witnessing the genocide. The process of moral remembering thus placed a large share of guilt on actors, especially key states and institutions, outside of Rwanda. However, this guilt only concerned the specific events of 1994. What was, in a sense, *unremembered* in the aftermath of the genocide was the fact that the sharp ethnic separation between Hutus and Tutsis, which fueled the genocide, was to a large extent a remnant of the colonial system set up by Germany and Belgium in the nineteenth and twentieth centuries. While this line of interpretation was surely available and voiced by numerous observers, the mainstream memory process gravitated around the genocide in a narrower fashion. Another major moral memory, the Srebrenica massacre in 1995 during the Balkan Wars, holds a related story of amnesia and erasure. The massacre had a clear perpetrator in the form of the Bosnian-Serb army under Ratko Mladic. Yet, the event and its establishment as a moral memory have resulted in a portrait of Serbia and Serbians as inherently villainous. While such an attribution of guilt was rooted in observable facts, it does, however, risk creating a one-sided remembering of a conflict in which atrocities were committed not only by the Serbs and in which not all Serbians endorsed nationalist policies. Interestingly, some individuals, organizations, and parties at the *national level* in Serbia fiercely contest the global moral memories surrounding the Balkan Wars and Serbia's role in it. While Ratko Mladic has acquired the status as a kind of *negative global icon*, he is viewed as a positive icon and hero in some quarters in Serbia. In fact, it might be argued that the villainization of Serbia has fueled the formation of national counter-narratives and *counter-symbols*. Related processes have been and are occurring in Turkey over the Armenian genocide and in Japan over the Nanking massacre.

### ADAPTATION AND SELF-CELEBRATION

The book has consistently argued that global injustice symbols are carriers of values and meanings. These values and meanings do not flow more or less automatically from the objects subjected to political symbolization: they are imputed by human actors and through political action. This implies that while the study of symbols is the study of the events surrounding the empirical objects underlying them, it is also, at a different level, the study of those infusing such objects with meaning. In chapter 5 on Neda Agha Soltan and dramatic diffusion, part of the analysis revolved around the way Neda was interpreted from within an existing and globally available political-cultural schema morally and politically contrasting Iran and the West. This led to an amplification and perhaps even exaggeration of certain aspects of Neda and the circumstances surrounding her death. For example, Neda's fate was widely interpreted as related to gender issues and the suppression of women within Iran and Islam in general. The chapter's argument was not that such an interpretation was unsubstantiated but rather that it rested on rather limited empirical facts. What the case of Neda consequently indicates is how symbolic processes entail elements of *adaptation* in which the symbolized object is fitted to existing interpretive schemas and thus to the moral and political visions and expectations of those actors imputing the object with meaning. These actors are often rooted in the West. The individuals elevated to iconic status are thus individuals who represent Western values and, consequently, are seen as a light in the backwardness of a South in which undemocratic, nationalistic, and fundamentalist forces still hold sway. Malala Yousafzai achieved global iconic status during 2012 because of her commitment to the struggle for gender equality, which is widely seen as a hallmark of the Western democratic experience and one of the values we employ to distinguish ourselves from less-developed and not fully modern societies. Malala thus represents the forces in that part of the world that ultimately strive to be like "us." Pursuing this line of inquiry and critique, it is notable how global injustice symbols involve elements of *self-celebration* on the part of the meaning-imputing agents and audiences. When Mandela's release was celebrated at Wembley Stadium in 1990, in the first instance, of course, it was a celebration of his release and the impending end of apartheid. But there was also an undercurrent of self-celebration in which the release of Mandela was attributed to the antiapartheid movement and global society in general. These observations, importantly, allow us to address potential North-South inequalities in relation to global injustice symbols. It is thus evident that most of the best-known global symbols have a Southern origin. Yet the actors and audiences imputing these with meaning are predominantly Western. This is not a problem per se as it is a process that also reveals a positive global extension of chains of responsibility and caring. It does nevertheless raise significant concerns over the realities of a global society as it paints a picture of a world in which North-South power inequalities persist at the level of global moral and political meaning making.

UNEVENNESS AND THE LOCAL-NATIONAL-GLOBAL NEXUS

Pointing to the global nature of injustice symbols does not, as noted in the "Division and Contestation" subsection, imply harmony. Nor does it imply *homogeneity* in the sense that global injustice symbols are evenly distributed on a global scale. In reality many of them are anchored more powerfully in some countries and regions than in others. The discussion on adaptation and self-celebration already indicates a certain geographic bias in which global injustice symbols are shaped through global social movements with a predominant basis in the West and given meaning through political-cultural schemas originating in this part of the world. Of course, this is not to say that global injustice symbols are constructs of the West and anchored only in the West. Considering the cases of Mandela and Rwanda, for example, these symbols have special significance in the African region: the Rwandan genocide because it directly affected several other states as a result of huge flows of refugees and Mandela because the colonial experience in which he and apartheid was grounded is widely shared across the region. Nevertheless, these examples also point to the uneven character of the distribution of global injustice symbols. For example, it is expectable that Mandela is less known in the Asian and South American region as compared to Africa, Europe, and the United States. Similarly, Salvador Allende, who died in the violent takeover by Augusto Pinochet in Chile in 1973, has significant status as an injustice symbol in South American history and collective memory as well as in Europe and the United States where numerous actors engaged in solidarity activities with Chile (states in this part of the world also welcomed and received a strong flow of refugees). His status is undoubtedly less pronounced in, say, Africa and Asia. The above observation primarily points at uneven distribution of *knowledge*. Closely related to this is the issue of unevenness in *meaning attribution*. It was already mentioned how the Mandela icon is understood and interpreted in the context of the colonial experience. Mandela thus represents the wider struggle against white colonialism during much of the twentieth century. This understanding does not stand in contradiction to the meanings associated with Mandela outside the African region. But since audiences in Europe and the United States do not have immediate experiences as victims of colonialism, Mandela is also interpreted in a more general sense as a symbol of a universal struggle for democracy and human rights. Such unevenness in meaning attribution is even more prominent in the case of Guantanamo Bay, which in the West is interpreted primarily through a human rights political-cultural schema, whereas at least some actors in the Muslim world interpret it through a political Islamist schema. While the above has focused on regional differences, it is equally pertinent to underline how some global symbols may have a certain national bias. The Rwandan genocide, for example, is more firmly anchored in Belgian and French memory because of these countries' present and historical relationship and involvement with Rwanda. In a different dynamic, some injustice symbols are more or less erased or contested in the countries considered responsible for the originating events. This was alluded to above in the status of Ratko Mladic in Serbia. And in chapter 5 on Neda Agha Soltan it was discussed how authorities in Iran worked hard to *de-symbolize* and thus to politically erase or at least downplay the death of Neda within Iran.

## THE GLOBAL CIVIL SPHERE

As noted and discussed in chapter 1, Alexander (2006) has developed the concept of the civil sphere as an alternative to that of civil society. Traditionally, civil society has been conceived of as non-state areas of private and public life, that is the family, the market, and, in the Toquevillean tradition, voluntary associations. Rather than reducing civil society to certain kinds of activities and actors, Alexander argues that we should think of civil society, from a Durkheimian perspective, as "a solidary sphere, in which a certain kind of universalizing community comes to be culturally defined and to some degree institutionally enforced" (Alexander, 2006: 31). This is what he refers to as the *civil sphere*. The civil sphere thus denotes the social anchoring of moral and political values such as solidarity, universalism, equality, democracy, and human rights. It is a moral-political ideational reservoir, which can be, and continuously is, employed to argue and fight against injustice. This is evident, for example, when the market in general and corporations in particular, are criticized for producing inequality and other effects considered morally and politically problematic. And it is seen when states are criticized for thinking and acting only or mainly on the basis of realist and strategic calculations. In both situations, we see a *universalizing* argument at play: one that insists on addressing and giving weight to ideals that transcend the *particularity* of, for example, state and corporate interests. The civil sphere and civil-sphere-based action cannot be reduced to specific actors, although Alexander (2006) seems to grant a special role to social movements and the media. In chapter 1, it was argued that it is necessary to understand social movements in a broader sense than what has been the norm within the field of social movement studies. This expansion rested on the argument that social movements should not be defined according to its actors but rather to a certain kind of *moral-political* action rooted in and productive of the civil sphere. One implication of this understanding is that states, institutions, and individuals may in some cases be part of social movements. As noted in chapter 1, for example, states may act not only on the basis of realist logic but also, potentially, on a moral-political logic (as in the antiapartheid movement discussed in chapter 2).

As Alexander (2007, 2012) has indicated, the concept of the civil sphere may be usefully extended to the global level, although he cautiously labels it as a *nascent* global civil sphere. While it is true, as briefly discussed in chapter 1, that the global civil sphere does not have the same degree of legal, institutional, and political anchoring as at the national level, this book and the findings summarized in the "Realities of Global Society" section, demonstrate that at an ideational level there is a rather well-established global civil sphere, not just a nascent one. The concepts of global society and a global civil sphere are closely related. Sociologically speaking, the civil sphere lies at the heart of society because it harbors many of the values that define how we see ourselves collectively, what unites us, and how we conceive of our individual and collective responsibilities toward others. From such a perspective, what characterizes globality is precisely the development of a global civil sphere in which solidaristic and universal values connect people and places morally and politically. It is a guiding argument of this book that global injustice symbols and social movements offer a fruitful empirical prism for studying and assessing the global civil sphere. At the beginning of the book it was argued that global social movement studies could benefit from a deeper theoretical engagement with value- and meaning-oriented strands in sociology. Reversely further development of the concept of the global civil sphere must place global social movements at the heart of such an exercise. While Alexander (2006) usefully acknowledges the role of social movements in producing and defending the civil sphere at the *national* level, he does not sufficiently illuminate this dynamic at the global level. This book, in contrast, has been premised on the theoretical argument that global social movements, broadly understood, are key actors in employing, reproducing, and extending values anchored in the global civil sphere. A civil sphere is not something carved into stone. It is a product of, and maintained through, human *action*. The moral-political action of social movements is central to deepening our understanding of this process.

Of course, to conclude that a global civil sphere exists is not to say that the world is one big happy family united around shared values and ideals. The evidence to the contrary is overwhelming as amply demonstrated in the "Limitations of Global Society" section. The observation of conflict, power relations, and biases, however, does not falsify the concept and theory of the global civil sphere. What it does indicate are two things that both qualify and to some extent even challenge the basic idea of a global civil sphere. First, as exemplified by the case of Guantanamo Bay and the global grievance community of political Islam (chapter 3), there are other political-cultural schemas available in the global public sphere than those anchored in the global civil sphere. The schema of political Islam enjoys great global resonance and is in some areas premised on nonuniversalizing ideas that are counter to, for example, the human rights and solidaristic values central in the global civil sphere (the political Islam schema does have a universalizing ambition, as evidenced in the concept of the Umma but this is a partial universality in that it only extends rights and concerns to Muslims). Contestation, competition, and challenge do not only come from political Islam but also from, especially, the realist and rational logic that informs state behavior. While states in some cases act on a moral-political logic, security interests dictate a realist behavior that often clash with and in many cases trump global civil-sphere-based action. This partly reflects the lack of strong institutional and legal enforcement mechanisms at the global level and exposes the fragility of the global civil sphere (and as such the importance of social movements in continuously defending it). Second, the observation of power and biases in the "Limitations of Global Society" section raises question marks over the concept and idea of a global civil sphere. Many of these observations point to Western dominance in global society: as seen in the way the Neda Agha Soltan symbol was adapted to a Western political-cultural schema, in how the freeing of Nelson Mandela involved a self-celebration of the West, and in the way the memory work surrounding the Rwandan genocide was characterized by some degree of amnesia. In other words, if we wish to maintain that a global civil sphere exists, this should be qualified so as to be able to identify how this sphere is predominantly Western based and maintained and developed by actors in this part of the world. In sum, it should be thought of as both contested and globally heterogeneous.

## Lessons for the Study of Global Social Movements

This book opened with the claim that research on global social movements, since its inception in the mid-1990s, has been characterized by a political-cultural and macro-sociological deficit. The predominant focus on institutions, resources, networks, and communication yields important theoretical and analytical insights but it does not have much to offer when it comes to the relationship between global social movements and global society. The book argues that because injustice symbols are powerful meaning and value carriers they provide a useful and almost unexplored prism for probing this relationship in an empirically grounded manner. In pursuing such an agenda, the book leans toward the cultural, dramatic, and emotional turn within social movement studies in the last couple of decades (see chapter 1). This literature, in contrast to most of the theoretical staples in the social movement field, that is, political opportunities, resources and organization, and framing, has not so far been adequately expanded to the study of global social movements. This book hopes to have shown that an expansion in such a direction is both needed and able to produce new political sociological insights. With its focus on injustice symbols as value and meaning carriers produced and employed in movement action, this book has, especially, sought to demonstrate the continued usefulness of late Durkheimian thinking for social movement studies in general and global social movement studies in particular. Viewing, as was done above, global social movements as related to and grounded in a *global civil sphere* is one way of addressing and illuminating this theoretical coupling of movements and society.

The core argument animating theorization and analysis in the book is that global injustice symbols are related to global social movements in a *dialectical* manner: global injustice symbols are the *outcomes* of global social movement activity and they offer ideational *resources* that can be employed in movement action. If we accept this dual argument, it becomes evident how global social movements do not simply *respond* to political events and situations but how they also *create* them through processes of meaning attribution and interpretation. It is in the latter capacity, and recalling the identification of a macrosociological deficit in the literature on global social movements, that they can and must be viewed as driving actors in the production of global society. As has been shown in the sections above, such production is not homogenous or harmonious: global injustice symbols, in varying degrees, involve and point to political conflict, biases, and power constellations at the global level. What is global about global injustice symbols, then, is consequently not that they are homogenously understood and distributed but rather the fact that they have been constructed in political processes and resonate for audiences that cannot be confined to the local or national level. It is hoped that future studies of global social movements will increasingly address the dynamics of value and meaning construction at a global level and the way global social movements are involved in them. Such an approach not only offers a new agenda for movement scholars but also opens up to ways of integrating the sometimes rather insular field of social movements with other sociological fields such as global sociology, cultural sociology, memory sociology, visual sociology, communication sociology, and development sociology.

It is worth noting in continuation of this argument that the conception of global social movements applied in this book is broader than in most accounts. It was thus argued in chapter 1 that the term should be expanded beyond activists and activist organizations. In all the cases analyzed in the book, the symbolic processes were thus driven by a multiplicity of actors (including activists, media, states, political parties, international institutions, artists, and networked citizens) converging around a common theme for shorter or longer periods of time and engaging in what was referred to in chapter 1 and in the "Global Civil Sphere" section as *moral-political action*. What united such a wide array of actors in all of the cases was thus a shared indignation over some event or situation involving perceived unjust human suffering. Action of this kind is moral-political because it builds on and reproduces collective values about just human behavior (the moral element) *and* is aimed to address, ameliorate, or prevent human suffering and injustice (the political element). It is believed that rethinking our unit of analysis in this way will broaden the empirical scope of the field in significant ways. This is an advancement in itself but it is also one with potential theoretical implications as it challenges the bulk of social movement theories, which have been developed mainly with activists and activist organizations in mind. This is not the time and place to engage with this challenge in full. But seen from the perspective of this book, the utility of an expansion along these lines is that it allows us to see that moral-political and civil-sphere-based action is not a monopoly of activism. With an emphasis on the type of action rather than on the type of actors, we place ourselves in a much better position to address the macro-sociological questions regarding the value and meaning, and hence society, producing potentials and capabilities of global social movements.

# Notes

## 1    Global Injustice Symbols

1. The literatures on global civil society and global social movements have developed rather separately. The global social movement literature was kickstarted in the mid- and late 1990s by scholars such as Jackie Smith (Smith, Chatfield, and Pagnucco, 1997), Kathryn Sikkink (Keck and Sikkink, 1998), Sidney Tarrow (1998), Donatella della Porta (della Porta and Kriesi, 1999), and Dieter Rucht (1999). As their theoretical guide, these works used tools developed for the study of national social movements, especially political opportunity theory, resource mobilization theory, and framing theory. Parallel with this, another group of scholars such as Mary Kaldor, Helmut Anheier, and Marlies Glasius (Anheier, Glasius, and Kaldor, 2001; Kaldor, 2003) were inspired by the same empirical phenomena, but focused research and analysis around the concept of civil society, which had been repopularized in the wake of the end of the Cold War (Cohen and Arato, 1992).

2. Symbols have not altogether escaped the attention of social movement scholars. A number of works broadly located within the Chicago School devote a good deal of attention to symbols and activism (e.g., Klapp, 1972; Lang and Lang, 1961; Turner and Killian, 1957). Social constructivist approaches gravitating around the concept of frame have also demonstrated sensitivity to the relationship (e.g., Benford and Snow, 2000; Gamson and Lasch, 1983; Gamson and Modigliani, 1989; Johnston, 2009; Keck and Sikkink, 1998; Zuo and Benford, 1995). And scholars who belong to the cultural turn in social movement theorizing similarly grant symbols some prominence (e.g., Emirbayer and Goodwin, 1996; Jasper, 1997; Jasper and Poulsen, 1995). Significant and inspiring as they are, these works also testify to the incomplete integration of a symbolic perspective in social movement research. First, the concept of symbol is all too often employed based on no or vague definitions. As will become painfully clear later, defining and delimiting the concept is a daunting task in its own right. The lack of clear definitions and extended conceptual discussion hampers the incorporation of the concept into the literature. It indirectly signals that it need not be taken seriously and provides a fragmented basis for further theoretical and conceptual development. Second, while symbols figure in many analyses,

they are never or only rarely at the center of the research agenda. Typically, they serve an auxiliary role, subsumed under wider research interests. As a result, symbols are too often treated as givens, leaving the complex and intriguing nature of injustice symbol formation inadequately explored. Third, to the extent that symbols have been employed in analyses, there has been a certain bias toward the instrumental and strategic side of the coin. Symbols are primarily viewed as elements in a Swidlerian cultural toolbox (Swidler, 1986); resources that can be mobilized to strengthen resonance and legitimacy and, ultimately, achieve desired goals. As the discussions that follow will demonstrate, the relevance of strategic approaches to symbols and social movements is not refuted. Rather, as elucidated later in the chapter, the aim is to extend it sociologically with the argument that social movements not only draw on *existing* symbols but also *create* them and how, as a consequence, they are centrally engaged in the "production" of society.

3. Related contestations over reality are found in the cases of Muhammad al-Durrah and Mohamed Bouazizi. Following the footage of Muhammad al-Durrah referred to in the "A Typology of Objects" subsection, the incident became embroiled in a fierce dispute over the facts. Allegations and suggestions emerged that the killing bullets were most likely not fired by Israeli forces (see, e.g., Fallows, 2003, for an account of the controversy) and that the footage had been manipulated by France 2 to garner sympathy for the Palestinian cause (see Enderlin, 2010, for a response to this allegation; Enderlin was bureau chief in Israel at the time of the incident and did the voiceover for the original footage that later circulated in the media worldwide). France 2 subsequently filed defamation suits against Philippe Karsenty, a French politician and the most outspoken critic of the footage and its presentation. This process only ended in 2013 with Karsenty being convicted of defamation by the Paris Court of Appeals. Mohamed Bouazizi's self-immolation case is discussed in detail in chapter 5 note 2.

4. The Abu Ghraib photographs offer another useful illustration of the de-symbolization dynamic. The now infamous photographs became headline news in 2004 and immediately gained iconic status. At one level, the documentary character of the photographs provided indisputable evidence of a situation that was legally indefensible and, for most people, also morally problematic. At another level, these facts lent themselves to different interpretations. US authorities immediately apologized for the incident, but promoted a "rotten apples" story emphasizing how Abu Ghraib was not representative for the United States and its army (Bennett, Lawrence, and Livingston, 2006), or, in the terminology of the preceding text, how the incidents constituted a particular problem and not a universal one. In effect, they were eagerly trying to *de-symbolize* Abu Ghraib, or perhaps more accurately, to remove its symbolic potential. Critics and enemies of the United States, in contrast, attempted to universalize the facts so as to turn Abu

Ghraib into a symbol of what was wrong about the war in Iraq, or, in a wider sense, with the United States as such.

## 2  POLITICAL ICONOGRAPHY

1. Some of these elements were negatively evident in the case of Rigoberta Menchú whose icon formation was halted by allegations that she had dramatized her biography. In 1984, Menchú, the daughter of an indigenous Guatemalan activist burned to death by the Guatemalan army in 1980, published a testimonial book based on a taped interview with Elisabeth Burgos-Debray (Menchú and Burgos-Debray, 1984). Gradually, and in parallel with a slow transition from military rule to democracy in Guatemala, Menchú became a key political figure in the country, combining claims for democracy with a struggle for new political and cultural rights for Guatemala's indigenous majority population. This coincided with a general assertion throughout Latin America of indigenous identity and rights. In 1991, Guatemala hosted a hemispheric conference commemorating five hundred years of indigenous resistance (as counted from the year of Columbus's arrival in the New World). This proved an effective launching pad for Menchú's awarding, in 1992, of the Nobel Peace Prize. Already a national icon of democracy and justice, the peace prize added a global dimension (Arias, 2001). The tainting and partial dismantling of her iconic status began in the late 1990s when American anthropologist David Stoll (1999) published a book that questioned a number of details given in Menchú's 1984 testimonial book. These concerned, among other things, Menchú's claims that she came from an impoverished family and that she had witnessed her brother being burnt to death in a politically motivated incident. Stoll's book sparked a great deal of controversy, with some even calling for a revocation of her Nobel Peace Prize (see Arias, 2001, for a collection of original material on the controversy as well as academic treatments of it). Menchú may not have lied in the sense of creating an entirely new account of her past but rather amplified and dramatized certain events and conditions (e.g., her brother was killed for political reasons but not burned, and her family was shown to be comparatively well-off). What is notable here is how these revelations were nevertheless able to question, in particular, her moral purity and the extent of personal sacrifice. The two elements weave together. By exaggerating certain key events and conditions in her life (and, hence, her degree of personal sacrifice), her moral purity was placed in serious doubt. It may be acceptable for others to amplify and dramatize certain aspects of the icon's life experience. When the icon or icon-in-the-making does so herself it is considered manipulative, strategic, self-interested, and, as such, incompatible with audience expectations for the iconic personae.

2. Alexander (2006: ch. 12; 2011: ch. 7) and McAdam (2000: 127) develop this point in their discussion of dramaturgy in the American civil rights

movement, arguing that the movement consciously sought to unleash repressive force. Birmingham, with its commissioner of public safety, "Bull" Connor, known for his racist attitudes and ill temper, was chosen as a key site for their 1963 campaign precisely for these reasons. As predicted, violent confrontations ensued. Media images, which spoke of excessive violence on the part of authorities, became news across the country and helped raise sympathy for the activists to new levels.

3. The Rivonia trial was so named after the Johannesburg suburb where South African police arrested 19 ANC and Umkhonto we Sizwe activists (many of them in leading positions) on July 11, 1963 (Umkhonto we Sizwe, Spear of the Nation, was the armed branch of the ANC; Umkhonto we Sizwe was formed partly in response to the banning of ANC in 1960). Mandela was not among this group as he had been arrested the year before. The group was accused of sabotage and several members condemned to life imprisonment.

4. The public platform of the Rivonia trial was visible beyond South Africa also as it was covered by several non–South African newspapers, especially in the United Kingdom. Mandela was not naive about the possibilities that this created. Anthony Sampson, a British writer and journalist, and later Mandela's biographer, with a long-standing relationship with the ANC, covered the trial for *Observer* and was asked personally by Mandela to comment on the speech and assess its impact potential on a global audience (Sampson, 1999). At least three further observations from the Rivonia speech indicate Mandela's sensitivity to global audiences: first, the speech goes to great lengths to ensure how the Umkhonto we Sizwe and the taking up of arms was a desperate last resort in the context of a repressive and petrified regime; second, Mandela appears concerned to distance himself, Umkhonto we Sizwe, and the ANC from the communists; and third, he continuously emphasizes how the struggle against apartheid is a struggle for democracy. While we should be cautious not to cast these observations in a purely strategic and calculated light, it is quite plausible that they were emphasized in order to maximize global resonance. Portraying himself as an armed fighter forced by intolerable injustice, a noncommunist, and an avowed democrat served to steer Umkhonto we Sizwe and the ANC clear of the Cold War ideological fault line and, thus, to place the antiapartheid struggle on a decidedly moral terrain palatable to wide audiences in, especially, Europe and the United States.

5. These activities not only included the work of political activists but also actions by states and international institutions. Most notably the global struggle against apartheid was given high priority within the UN from an early point. Based on the UN General Assembly Resolution 1761, the Special Committee on the Policies of Apartheid of the Government of the Republic of South Africa (later shortened to the Special Committee on Apartheid) started working in 1963 (see Stultz, 1991).

6. The general revitalization of antiapartheid activism in the mid-1970s had to some extent been facilitated by the widely publicized uprisings in Soweto in

1976, which involved several instances of often visually documented police brutality (e.g., Sanders, 2000: ch. 7; Thörn, 2006: ch. 7).

7. Sincere thanks to Håkan Thörn for providing this quotation, which is not included in Thörn (2006). The account has been verified in a recent personal correspondence (January 10, 2014) with Enuga S. Reddy.

8. According to Håkan Thörn (personal correspondence), Hollingsworth exaggerates the resistance from, especially the AAM, who, according to Thörn, had accepted and even suggested the idea of a major international tribute concert.

9. The survey combined broad searches on the Internet, on the various branches of Amazon, and in the major Danish library database. While the survey does not claim to be exhaustive, it does contain the large majority and most central of Mandela-related publications in major languages.

## 3 GRIEVANCE COMMUNITIES

1. Jihadist terrorism is terrorism based on a politicized and radicalized interpretation of Islam. The term is preferable to, for example, Islamic terrorism because the latter links a religion (Islam) with terrorism in a conceptually imprecise and normatively problematic way.

2. Interestingly, Obama's remarks have sparked some debate and controversy in the United States. Groups and commentators advocating for the preservation of the detention facility have, for example, argued that Guantanamo bay plays a rather insignificant role in al-Qaeda communications.

3. The Muhammad cartoons were the object of heated global social movement activity in January and February 2006 (Olesen, 2007a, 2007b, 2009). After the protests subsided, the cartoons have become established as a central injustice symbol within the political-cultural schema of political Islam. They have thus been appropriated, for example, by the world's leading jihadist organization, al-Qaeda, and are repeatedly cited as motivation and justification for actual or planned terrorist attacks. This tendency has not gone unnoticed by security analysts. In a 2009 report, the Danish police's intelligence service, PET (2009), published a report documenting the continuing presence of the Muhammad cartoons in al-Qaeda's communications (see Olesen, 2014, for an extended analysis along these lines).

4. IntelCenter, which has published and collected this and other al-Qaeda-related communiqués quoted in the paper, is a private company working closely with American authorities. Its main objective is the collection and publication of material produced and disseminated by jihadist terrorist organizations. The credibility of IntelCenter has been in doubt in a couple of situations in recent years, with allegations that the company manipulated jihadist videos to establish links with al-Qaeda and other terrorist organizations. Other critiques have focused on a lack of transparency in regard to how and where IntelCenter obtains some of the videos it publicizes. However, there is no reason to believe

that the communiqués cited in this chapter are not genuine, even if their origin is not clearly stated in all cases.

5. For analyses of Jihadist terrorism from a social movement perspective, see, for example, Beck (2008); Bergesen (2007); Gunning (2009); Snow and Byrd (2007).

6. It should be noted, importantly, that the Guantanamo critical movement cannot be contextualized only within the political-cultural schema of political Islam. First, criticism from many actors in the Muslim region has a political and human rights angle rather than a religious one (see, e.g., the work by the Islamic Human Rights Commission). Second, critical voices also come from the non-Muslim world (this theme is revisited in the chapter's conclusion).

7. As can be seen in this and other quotes, Abu Ghraib is spelled in various ways. In Arab the most common spellings are Abu Ghuraib and Abu Ghurayb.

8. As-Sahab is considered to be al-Qaeda's public relations branch; see, for example, Rogan (2007).

9. Bagram, or in military terms, Bagram Theater Internment Facility, is located in Afghanistan as part of Bagram Air Base.

### 4   MORAL MEMORIES

1. Global moral memories may be global without being simultaneously national. The Holocaust and apartheid continue to be hotly debated topics in their countries of origin. Yet, other injustice memories such as the Srebrenica massacre, Japanese atrocities in Nanking during the World War II, and the Turkish genocide of the Armenians in the early twentieth century remain largely taboo in Serbia, Japan, and Turkey despite their presence in debates outside these countries (see Alexander, 2012). Other injustice memories may be regional rather than global. For example, the massacre on Palestinian refugees in Sabra and Shatila in Lebanon in 1982 is probably anchored most strongly in the collective memories of Arab countries.

2. In the United States, the My Lai massacre in Vietnam in 1968 keeps resurfacing in contemporary debates about the United States' international military engagement. When US Marines killed 24 Iraqis, including women and children in Haditha, on November 19, 2005, the case quickly drew comparisons to My Lai. The comparison, however, was not uncontested. Those arguing against the analogy focused on the following facts: many more people (300–500) were killed at My Lai than at Haditha; the My Lai massacre took place over several hours whereas the one in Haditha occurred within a few minutes; and My Lai was the scene of systematic abuse (rape, torture) of villagers, while none such incidents took place in Haditha. Those making the analogy were less concerned with factual similarities. They saw Haditha as just another example of the morally unacceptable consequences of US military engagement (the killing of innocent civilians).

3. The residual mechanism was established in December 2010 "to finish the remaining tasks of the Tribunals for Rwanda and the Former Yugoslavia, and maintain their respective legacies" (UN, 2010).

4. A LexisNexis search, for the 1994–2011 period, based on the search term "International Criminal Tribunal for Rwanda" thus yields 478 newspaper articles and reports. The LexisNexis database primarily covers US, Canadian, and UK newspapers. The majority of reports appeared in the following publications: *New York Times* (44), *Toronto Star* (27), *Globe and Mail* (25), *Guardian* (23), *Gazette* (21), and *Washington Post* (17).

5. The full list of visitors can be obtained from the author on request.

6. Following the genocide, the media have also engaged in self-reflection about their coverage and how that may have played a part in delaying intervention. See Grzyb (2009) and Thompson (2007) for predominantly critical analyses of Western media coverage of the Rwandan genocide.

7. In a 2009 address to the parliament in Kosovo, former US president Bill Clinton stated that NATO's and the United States' military intervention in the conflict between Serbia and Kosovo in 1999 was significantly motivated by the failure of intervention in Rwanda five years earlier (BalkanInsight, 2009). And in early 2011, US secretary of state Hillary Clinton cited the failure of intervention in Rwanda in the debate over military intervention against Libya and Muammar Gadaffi (Harris, 2011).

8. Other films include *100 Days* (2001), *A Sunday in Kigali* (2006), *Shake Hands with the Devil* (2007), *Munyurangabo* (2007), and *Kinyarwanda* (2011).

9. Paul Rusesabagina received the US Presidential Medal of Freedom on November 9, 2005, from President George W. Bush.

10. Documentaries related to the Rwanda genocide include *Journey into Darkness* (1994); *A Culture of Murder* (1994); *The Bloody Tricolor* (1995); *Valentina's Story* (1997); *When Good Men Do Nothing* (1997); *Triumph of Evil* (1998); *Keepers of Memory* (2004); *Shake Hands with the Devil: The Journey of Roméo Dallaire* (2004); *Ghosts of Rwanda* (2005); *Flower in the Gun Barrel* (2009), and *A Generation after Genocide* (2010).

11. The UNAMIR was created to aid the implementation of the Arusha Accords (August 4, 1993), signed to end the civil war in Rwanda.

## 5  Dramatic Diffusion

1. According to early accounts Bouazizi was a college graduate; this has later been dismissed (see, e.g., France 2, 2012).

2. Obviously, the establishment of injustice and innocence are ongoing processes that may be impacted by the availability of new information or by authorities' attempt at de-symbolization. In the case of Bouazizi, contestation has happened at two levels. First, as noted in the text, the main reason for Bouazizi's self-immolation was supposed to have been the humiliating slap in the face by a female municipal inspection officer, Faida Hamdi. Hamdi was

subsequently jailed, yet acquitted some four months later. Hamdi has later emerged to not only deny the infamous slap but to also portray Bouazizi as the main aggressor in the altercation (France 2, 2012; Totten, 2012). No one has been able to verify any of these diverging accounts. Yet, nevertheless, the result seems to have been a partial role reversal as Hamdi has also explained how she was jailed by the Ben Ali regime as a scapegoat and to deflect anger away from the regime. Recalling the arguments made earlier that injustice symbols build on victim *innocence*, claims such as these pose a direct challenge to the moral status of the Bouazizi injustice symbol. Second, there are signs, especially at the local level of Sidi Bouzid, that Bouazizi's status as injustice symbol is not as uncomplicated as it once was. In Sidi Bouzid rumors have been spreading that Bouazizi's mother, Manoubia, has received money from international institutions and media and that she and her family have been capitalizing on Bouazizi's death. Apparently driven from the city by increasing hostility, the family now lives in the city of La Marsa near the capital of Tunis, further fueling the rumors (Abouzeid, 2011; Sengupta, 2011). While Faida Hamdi's intervention involves a direct attack on Bouazizi's moral character and innocence, the criticism of his mother and family is an indirect attack. While personal injustice symbols presuppose moral purity on part of the background person, this moral purity can be posthumously tarnished by the actions of those considered to be its custodians. Whether these rumors contain some truth or are expressions of jealously is unclear and perhaps not important. What matters is that they are out there and apparently taking root in the negotiations over Bouazizi's legacy.

3. The Basij is a paramilitary unit working with the Iranian regime and the Revolutionary Guard. During suppression of the 2009 protests, Basij members on motorbikes played a key role in the violence against and intimidation of protesters.

4. The basis of this widespread comparison is somewhat unclear as Joan of Arc was not involved in a democratic struggle per se. It thus seems to refer, in a more general sense, to the fact that Joan of Arc died as a result of her refusal to compromise her fundamental (religious) beliefs.

5. This observation is, however, partly contradicted (but not verified by other sources consulted during the research) by Caspian Makan, Neda's boyfriend, who has noted, "She was a natural leader and attracted many [protesters] to her side. I think that is why she was shot. The Iranian state and its security officials did not want her, they wanted to extinguish her" (quoted in Athanasiadis, 2009).

6. When Oxford University in 2009 created a scholarship in the name of Neda Agha Soltan, the Iranian regime in a de-symbolization attempt protested in a letter stating that the university was undermining its scientific credibility.

7. Universalization was expressed, for example, in an initiative by Iranian photographer Reza Deghati in which protesters in cities around the world held

up placards with Neda's face over their own (see Iran Freedom Caravans, 2009), symbolically assuming her identity (Andén-Papadopoulos, 2014).

8. See http://www.youtube.com/watch?v=xL6hpf20sAQ, accessed January 14, 2014.

9. Among these is one made by her boyfriend, Caspian Makan, http://www.youtube.com/watch?v=9guTS2YFrRg, accessed January 3, 2014.

# REFERENCES

Abouzeid, R. (2011). "Mohamed Bouazizi's Unexpected Sequel: A Tunisian Soap Opera," *Time*, December 14, http://content.time.com/time/specials/packages/article/0,28804,2101745_2102138_2102235,00.html, accessed January 5, 2012.

Aegis (2007). "London Societies Launch," http://www.aegistrust.org/index.php/Aegis-Rwanda/london-societies-launch.html, accessed September 11, 2013.

Aksu, E. (2009). "Global Collective Memory: Conceptual Difficulties of an Appealing Idea," *Global Society* 23(3): 317–332.

Alexander, J. C. (2004a). "Cultural Pragmatics: Social Performances between Ritual and Strategy," *Sociological Theory* 22(4): 527–573.

Alexander, J. C. (2004b). "Toward a Theory of Cultural Trauma," in J. C. Alexander, R. Eyerman, B. Giesen, N. J. Smelser, and P. Sztompka (eds.), *Cultural Trauma and Collective Identity* (Berkeley: University of California Press), pp. 1–30.

Alexander, J. C. (2004c). "On the Social Construction of Moral Universals: The 'Holocaust' from War Crime to Trauma Drama," in J. C. Alexander, R. Eyerman, B. Giesen, N. J. Smelser, and P. Sztompka (eds.), *Cultural Trauma and Collective Identity* (Berkeley: University of California Press), pp. 196–263.

Alexander, J. C. (2004d). "From the Depths of Despair: Performance, Counterperformance, and 'September 11,'" *Sociological Theory* 22(1): 88–105.

Alexander, J. C. (2006). *The Civil Sphere* (Oxford: Oxford University Press).

Alexander, J. C. (2007). "'Globalization' as Collective Representation: The New Dream of a Cosmopolitan Civil Sphere," in I. Rossi (ed.), *Frontiers of Globalization Research: Theoretical and Methodological Approaches* (New York: Springer), pp. 271–282.

Alexander, J. C. (2010). *The Performance of Politics: Obama's Victory and the Democratic Struggle for Power* (Oxford: Oxford University Press).

Alexander, J. C. (2011). *Performance and Power* (Oxford: Polity).

Alexander, J. C. (2012). *Trauma: A Social Theory* (Oxford: Polity).

Alexander, J. C., and R. N. Jacobs (1998). "Mass Communication, Ritual, and Civil Society," in T. Liebes and J. Curran (eds.), *Media, Ritual, and Identity* (London and New York: Routledge), pp. 23–41.

Alexander, J. C., and P. Smith (2003). "The Strong Program in Cultural Sociology: Elements of a Structural Hermeneutics," in J. C. Alexander (ed.), *The Meanings of Social Life: A Cultural Sociology* (Oxford: Oxford University Press), pp. 11–26.

Alexander, J. C., and J. L. Mast (2006). "Introduction: Symbolic Action in Theory and Practice: The Cultural Pragmatics of Symbolic Action," in J. C. Alexander,

B. Giesen, and J. L. Mast (eds.), *Social Performance: Symbolic Action, Cultural Pragmatics, and Ritual* (Cambridge: Cambridge University Press), pp. 1–28.

Alexander, J. C., D. Bartmanski, and B. Giesen (eds.) (2012). *Iconic Power: Materiality and Meaning in Social Life* (New York: Palgrave Macmillan).

Allan, S., and E. Thorsen (2009). *Citizen Journalism: Global Perspectives* (New York: Peter Lang).

al-Libi, A. (2007). "Confronting the War of Prisons," http://triceratops.brynmawr.edu:8080/dspace/bitstream/handle/10066/5030/ALL20070525.pdf? sequence=3, accessed March 10, 2011.

al-Libi, A. Y. (2009). "Iraq: between Indications of Victory and Conspiratorial Intrigues," in *Words of Abu Yahya al-Libi*, Vol. 1 (Alexandria, VA: IntelCenter), pp. 41–51.

al-Zawahiri, A. (2008a). "Video Statement," in *IntelCenter Terrorism Incident Reference (TIR): Afghanistan 2000–2007* (Alexandria, VA: IntelCenter), pp. 117–118.

al-Zawahiri, A. (2008b). "Letter to the Americans: Why Do We Fight and Resist You?," in *Words of Ayman al-Zawahiri*, Vol. 1 (Alexandria, VA: IntelCenter), pp. 70–79.

al-Zawahiri, A. (2008c). "Video Interview," in *Words of Ayman al-Zawahiri*, Vol. 1 (Alexandria, VA: IntelCenter), pp. 24–41.

al-Zawahiri, A. (2008d). "The Alternative Is Da'wa and Jihad" (Video Statement), in *Words of Ayman al-Zawahiri*, Vol. 1 (Alexandria, VA: IntelCenter), pp. 86–93.

al-Zawahiri, A. (2008e). "Video Interview," in *Words of Ayman al-Zawahiri*, Vol. 1 (Alexandria, VA: IntelCenter), pp. 6–15.

al-Zawahiri, A. (2008f). "Realities of the Conflict between Islam and Unbelief," in *Words of Ayman al-Zawahiri*, Vol. 1 (Alexandria, VA: IntelCenter), pp. 173–194.

Amnesty International (2008). "Guantanamo: Symbol of Wider Injustice," http://www.amnesty.org/en/library/asset/AMR51/005/2008/en/2ff74689-c5d6-11dc-9af1-b1d22f3b300e/amr510052008eng.pdf, accessed April 26, 2011.

Amnesty International (2013). http://www.amnesty.org/en/region/iran, accessed May 24, 2013.

Andén-Papadopoulos, K. (2014). "Citizen Camera-Witnessing: Embodied Political Dissent in the Age of 'Mediated Mass Self-Communication,'" *New Media and Society* 16(5): 753–769.

Anderson, B. (1983). *Imagined Communities: Reflections on the Origins and Speed of Nationalism* (London: Verso).

Anheier, H. K., M. Glasius, and M. Kaldor (2001). "Introducing Global Civil Society," in H. Anheier, M. Glasius, and M. Kaldor (eds.), *Global Civil Society Yearbook 2001* (Oxford: Oxford University Press), pp. 3–22.

Anheier, H. K., and N. Themudo (2002). "Organizational Forms of Global Civil Society: Implications of Going Global," in M. Glasius, M. Kaldor, and H. K. Anheier (eds.), *Global Civil Society Yearbook 2002* (Oxford: Oxford University Press), pp. 191–216.

Annan, K. (2004). "Rwanda Genocide 'Must Leave Us Always with a Sense of Bitter Regret and Abiding Sorrow', Says Secretary-General to New York Memorial

Conference," March 26, http://www.un.org/News/Press/docs/2004/sgsm9223. doc.htm, accessed June 13, 2011.

Arias, A. (ed.) (2001). *The Rigoberta Menchú Controversy* (Minneapolis: University of Minnesota Press).

Assmann, A., and C. Assmann (2010). "Neda: The Career of a Global Icon," in A. Assmann and S. Conrad (eds.), *Memory in a Global Age: Discourses, Practices, and Trajectories* (Houndmills: Palgrave Macmillan), pp. 225–242.

Athanasiadis, I. (2009). "Exclusive: Boyfriend Speaks of His Love for Neda Agha Soltan, Murdered Iranian Protester," *The Observer*, November 15, http://www.guardian.co.uk/world/2009/nov/15/neda-agha-soltan, accessed 3 June 2013.

Ayoob, M. (2008). *The Many Faces of Political Islam: Religion and Politics in the Muslim World* (Ann Arbor: University of Michigan Press).

Baghat, G. (2003). "Iran, the United States, and the War on Terrorism," *Studies in Conflict & Terrorism*, 26(2): 93–104.

Baghat, G. (2006). "Nuclear Proliferation: The Islamic Republic of Iran," *Iranian Studies* 39(3): 307–327.

BalkanInsight (2009). "Clinton: Rwanda Guilt Led to Kosovo Intervention," November 2, http://www.balkaninsight.com/en/article/clinton-rwanda-guilt-led-to-kosovo-intervention, accessed June 12, 2011.

Barnard, Rita (2014). "Introduction," in Rita Barnard (ed.), *The Cambridge Companion to Nelson Mandela* (New York: Cambridge University Press), pp. 1–26.

Bartmanski, D., and J. C. Alexander (2012). "Materiality and Meaning in Social Life: Toward an Iconic Turn in Cultural Sociology," in J. C. Alexander, Dominik Bartmanski, and Bernhard Giesen (eds.), *Iconic Power: Materiality and Meaning in Social Life* (New York: Palgrave Macmillan), pp. 1–12.

BBC (2006). "Zawahiri Addresses Afghans—Excerpts," June 22, http://news.bbc.co.uk/2/hi/south_asia/5106330.stm, accessed May 5, 2012.

BBC (2009). "Neda: An Iranian Martyr" (Documentary), November 24, http://www.youtube.com/watch?v=C4-iLG6FwRc, accessed June 14, 2013.

Beardsley, B. (2009). "Lessons Learned or Not Learned from the Rwandan Genocide," in A. F. Grzyb (ed.), *The World and Darfur: International Response to Crimes against Humanity in Western Sudan* (Montreal: McGill-Queen's University Press), pp. 41–60.

Beck, C. J. (2008). "The Contribution of Social Movement Theory to Understanding Terrorism," *Sociology Compass* 2(5): 1565–1581.

Beissinger, M. R. (2007). "Structure and Example in Modular Political Phenomena: The Diffusion of Bulldozer/Rose/Orange/Tulip Revolutions," *Perspectives on Politics* 5:259–276.

Bell, D. (ed.) (2006a). *Memory, Trauma and World Politics: Reflections on the Relationship between Past and Present* (Houndmills: Palgrave Macmillan).

Bell, D. (2006b). "Introduction: Memory, Trauma and World Politics," in D. Bell (ed.), *Memory, Trauma and World Politics: Reflections on the Relationship between Past and Present* (Houndmills: Palgrave Macmillan), pp. 1–29.

Bellah, R. N. (ed.) (1973). *Emile Durkheim on Morality and Society* (Chicago: Chicago University Press).

Benford, R. D., and D. A. Snow (2000). "Framing Processes and Social Movements: An Overview and Assessment," *Annual Review of Sociology* 26:611–639.

Bennett, W. L. (1983/2005). *News: The Politics of Illusion* (New York: Longman).

Bennett, W. L., R. G. Lawrence, and S. Livingston (2006). "None Dare Call It Torture: Indexing and the Limits of Press Independence in the Abu Ghraib Scandal," *Journal of Communication* 56(3): 467–485.

Bennett, W. L., and A. Segerberg (2012). "The Logic of Connective Action: Digital Media and the Personalization of Contentious Politics," *Information, Communication and Society* 15(5): 739–768.

Bergesen, A. J. (2007). "A Three-Step Model of Terrorist Violence," *Mobilization* 12(2): 111–118.

bin Laden, O. (2008). "Audio Statement," in *Words of Osama bin Laden*, Vol. 1 (Alexandria, VA: IntelCenter), pp. 79–92.

Bob, C. (2005). *The Marketing of Rebellion: Insurgents, Media, and International Activism* (Cambridge: Cambridge University Press).

Boli, J., and G. M. Thomas (eds.) (1999). *Constructing World Culture: International Nongovernmental Organizations since 1875* (Stanford, CA: Stanford University Press).

Boltanski, L. (1999). *Distant Suffering: Morality, Media and Politics* (Cambridge: Cambridge University Press).

Booth, W. J. (2006). *Communities of Memory: On Witness, Identity, and Justice* (Ithaca, NY: Cornell University Press).

Borzou, D. (2009). "Family, Friends Mourn 'Neda,' Iranian Woman Who Died on Video," *Los Angeles Times*, June 23, http://www.latimes.com/news/nation world/world/la-fg-iran-neda23-2009jun23,0,366975,full.story, accessed June 8, 2013.

Bowker, D., and D. Kaye (2007). "Guantánamo by the Numbers," *New York Times*, November 13.

Buettner, A. (2011). *Holocaust Images and Picturing Catastrophe: The Cultural Politics of Seeing* (Farnham: Ashgate).

Burnet, J. E. (2009). "Whose Genocide? Whose Truth? Representations of Victim and Perpetrator in Rwanda," in A. L. Hinton and K. L. O'Neill (eds.), *Genocide: Truth, Memory, and Representation* (Durham, NC: Duke University Press), pp. 80–110.

Butler, J. (2004). *Precarious Life: The Powers of Mourning and Violence* (London and New York: Verso).

Butler, J. (2010). *Frames of War: When Is Life Grievable?* (London: Verso).

Byman, D. (2008). "Iran, Terrorism, and Weapons of Mass Destruction," *Studies in Conflict & Terrorism*, 31(3): 169–181.

Campbell, D. (2002). "Atrocity, Memory, Photography: Imaging the Concentration Camps of Bosnia—the Case of ITN versus Living Marxism (Part 1)," *Journal of Human Rights* 1(1): 1–33.

Campbell, Joseph (1949). *The Hero with a Thousand Faces* (Princeton, NJ, and Oxford, UK: Princeton University Press).

Caplan, G. (2009). "What Darfur Teaches Us about the Lessons Learned from Rwanda," in A. F. Grzyb (ed.), *The World and Darfur: International Response to Crimes against Humanity in Western Sudan* (Montreal: McGill-Queen's University Press), pp. 29–40.

Carvin, S. (2010). *Prisoners of America's Wars: From the Early Republic to Guantanamo* (New York: Columbia University Press).

Castells, M. (2012). *Networks of Outrage and Hope: Social Movements in the Internet Age* (Oxford: Polity).

Chabot, S. (2010). "Dialogue Matters: Beyond the Transmission Model of Transnational Diffusion between Movements," in R. K. Givan, K. M. Roberts, and S. A. Soule (eds.), *The Diffusion of Social Movements: Actors, Mechanisms, and Political Effects* (Cambridge: Cambridge University Press), pp. 99–124.

Chabot, S., and J. W. Duyvendak (2002). "Globalization and Transnational Diffusion between Social Movements: Reconceptualizing the Dissemination of the Gandhian Repertoire and the 'Coming Out' Routine," *Theory and Society* 31(6): 697–740.

Chouliaraki, L. (2006). *The Spectatorship of Suffering* (London: Sage).

Clinton, B. (1998). "Text of Clinton's Rwanda Speech," March 25, http://www.cbsnews.com/stories/1998/03/25/world/main5798.shtml, accessed June 1, 2011.

CNN (2009). "CNN Larry King Live: Interview with Iranian President Mahmoud Ahmadinejad" (Transcript), September 25, http://transcripts.cnn.com/TRANSCRIPTS/0909/25/lkl.01.html, accessed June 2, 2103.

Cohen, J. L., and A. Arato (1992). *Civil Society and Political Theory* (Cambridge, MA: MIT Press).

Conway, B. (2008). "Local Conditions, Global Environment and Transnational Discourses in Memory Work: The Case of Bloody Sunday (1972)," *Memory Studies* 1(2): 187–209.

Corman, S. R. (2009). "Guantanamo and al Qaeda Strategic Communication," *COMOPS Journal*, http://csc.asu.edu/2009/05/26/guantanamo-and-al-qaeda-strategic-communication/ , accessed November 12, 2013.

Crack, A. (2008). *Global Communication and Transnational Public Spheres* (New York: Palgrave Macmillan).

Crone, M., U. P. Gad, and M. K. Sheikh (2008). "Review Essay: Dusting for Fingerprints: The Aarhus Approach to Islamism," *Distinktion* 17:189–203.

Cubitt, G. (2007). *History and Memory* (Manchester: Manchester University Press).

Culverson, D. R. (1996). "The Politics of Anti-Apartheid Activism in the United States, 1969–1986," *Political Science Quarterly* 111(1): 127–149.

Dallaire, R. (2003). *Shake Hands with the Devil: The Failure of Humanity in Rwanda* (New York: Random House).

Dallaire, R. (2004). "Looking at Darfur, Seeing Rwanda," *New York Times*, October 4.

d'Anjou, L., and J. Van Male (1998). "Between Old and New: Social Movements and Cultural Change," *Mobilization* 3(2): 207–226.

Dayan, D., and E. Katz (1992), *Media Events: The Live Broadcasting of History* (Cambridge, MA: Harvard University Press).

de Soto, H. (2011). "The Real Mohamed Bouazizi," *Foreign Policy*, December 16.

Deghan, S. K. (2013). "Iran Elections: Death of Neda Agha-Soltan Haunts Voters," *Guardian*, June 13, http://www.theguardian.com/world/2013/jun/13/iran-elections-neda-agha-soltan, accessed 23 May 2014.

Deibert, R. J. (1997). *Parchment, Printing, and Hypermedia: Communication in World Order Transformation* (New York: Columbia University Press).

della Porta, D., and H. Kriesi (1999). "Social Movements in a Globalizing World: An Introduction," in D. della Porta, H. Kriesi, and D. Rucht (eds.), *Social Movements in a Globalizing World* (Houndmills and London: Macmillan), pp. 3–22.

della Porta, D., H. Kriesi, and D. Rucht (eds.) (1999). *Social Movements in a Globalizing World* (Houndmills and London: Macmillan).

della Porta, D., and S. Tarrow (eds.) (2005). *Transnational Protest and Global Activism* (Lanham, MD: Rowman and Littlefield).

della Porta, D., M. Andretta, L. Mosca, and H. Reiter (2006). *Globalization from Below: Transnational Activists and Protest Networks* (Minneapolis: University of Minnesota Press).

Durkheim, É. (1912/2001). *The Elementary Forms of Religious Life* (Oxford: Oxford University Press).

Edkins, J. (2003). *Trauma and the Memory of Politics* (Cambridge: Cambridge University Press).

Eko, L. (2012). *New Media, Old Regimes: Case Studies in Comparative Communication Law and Policy* (Plymouth: Lexington Books).

Elder, C. D., and R. W. Cobb (1983). *The Political Uses of Symbols* (New York and London: Longman).

Elman, P. (n.d.). "Nelson Mandela 70th Birthday Tribute," http://tonyhollings worth.com/?q=content/nelson-mandela-70th-birthday-tribute, accessed June 22, 2013.

Emirbayer, M. (1996). "Useful Durkheim," *Sociological Theory* 14(2): 109–130.

Emirbayer, M., and J. Goodwin (1996). "Symbols, Positions, Objects: Toward a New Theory of Revolutions and Collective Action," *History and Theory* 35(3): 358–374.

Enderlin, C. (2010). *Un enfant est mort: Netzarim, 30 septembre 2000* (Paris: Don Quichotte).

Evans, G., and S. Ellis (2004). "The Rwandan Genocide: Memory Is Not Enough," April 8, http://www.crisisgroup.org/en/regions/africa/central-africa/rwanda/the-rwandan-genocide-memory-is-not-enough.aspx, accessed May 25, 2011.

Eyerman, R. (2004). "Cultural Trauma: Slavery and the Formation African American Identity," in J. C. Alexander, R. Eyerman, B. Giesen, N. J. Smelser, and P. Sztompka (eds.), *Cultural Trauma and Collective Identity* (Berkeley: University of California Press), pp. 60–111.

Eyerman, R. (2006). "Performing Opposition or, How Social Movements Move," in J. C. Alexander, B. Giesen, and J. L. Mast (eds.), *Social Performance: Symbolic Action, Cultural Pragmatics, and Ritual* (Cambridge: Cambridge University Press), pp. 193–217.

Eyerman, R., J. C. Alexander, and E. B. Breese (2011). *Narrating Trauma: On the Impact of Collective Suffering* (Boulder, CO: Paradigm).

Fallows, J. (2003). "Who Shot Mohammed al-Dura?," *Atlantic Monthly*, June.

Fieldhouse, R. (2005). *Anti-Apartheid: A History of the Movement in Britain* (London: Merlin).

First, R. (1965/1973). "Foreword to the 1973 Edition," in *Nelson Mandela, No Easy Walk to Freedom* (London: Heinemann), pp. v–vii.

Flam, H., and D. King (eds.) (2005). *Emotions and Social Movements* (London and New York: Routledge).

France 2 (2012). "Mohamed Bouazizi, l'étincelle de la révolution, un an après," https://www.youtube.com/watch?v=twdNoBtMTSA, accessed December 16, 2012.

Fraser, N. (1992). "Rethinking the Public Sphere: A Contribution to the Critique of Actually Existing Democracy," in C. Calhoun (ed.), *Habermas and the Public Sphere* (Cambridge, MA: MIT Press), pp. 109–142.

Fraser, N. (1995). "Politics, Culture, and the Public Sphere: Toward a Postmodern Conception," in L. Nicholson and S. Seidman (eds.), *Social Postmodernism: Beyond Identity Politics* (Cambridge: Cambridge University Press), pp. 287–313.

Gamson, W. (1995). "Constructing Social Protest," in H. Johnston and B. Klandermans (eds.), *Social Movements and Culture* (Minneapolis: Regents of the University of Minnesota), pp. 85–106.

Gamson, W. A., and K. E. Lasch (1983). "The Political Culture of Social Welfare Policy," in S. E. Spiro and E. Yuchtman-Yaar (eds.), *Evaluating the Welfare State: Social and Political Perspectives* (New York: Academic), pp. 397–415.

Gamson, W., and A. Modigliani (1989). "Media Discourse and Public Opinion on Nuclear Power: A Constructionist Approach," *American Journal of Sociology* 95(1): 1–37.

Gamson, W. A., and G. Wolfsfeld (1993). "Movements and Media as Interacting Systems," *Annals of the American Academy of Political and Social Science* 528:114–125.

Garofalo, R. (1992). "Nelson Mandela, the Concerts: Mass Culture as Contested Terrain," in R. Garofalo (ed.), *Rockin' the Boat: Mass Music and Mass Movements* (Boston, MA: South End), pp. 55–65.

Geertz, C. (1973). *Interpretation of Cultures* (New York: Basic Books).

Gerges, F. A. (2005). *The Far Enemy: Why Jihad Went Global* (Cambridge: Cambridge University Press).

Giddens, A. (1991). *Modernity and Self-Identity* (Cambridge, UK: Polity).

Glaser, B. G., and A. L. Strauss (1967). *The Discovery of Grounded Theory* (Chicago: Aldine).

Goldberg, V. (1991). *The Power of Photography: How Photographs Changed Our Lives* (New York: Abbeville).

Goodman, T. (2011). *Staging Solidarity: Truth and Reconciliation in a New South Africa* (Boulder, CO: Paradigm).

Goodwin, J., and J. M. Jasper (1999). "Caught in a Winding, Snarling Vine: The Structural Bias of Political Process Theory," *Sociological Forum* 14(1): 27–54.

Goodwin, J., J. M. Jasper, and F. Polletta (eds.) (2001). *Passionate Politics: Emotions and Social Movements* (Chicago: University of Chicago Press).

Gorman, G. (2009). "Iranian Leaders Blaming CIA, Protestors, for Killing Neda," *ABC News*, June 26, http://abcnews.go.com/blogs/politics/2009/06/iranian-leaders-blaming-cia-protestors-for-killing-neda, accessed June 10, 2013.

Gray, T., and B. Martin (2008). "My Lai: The Struggle over Outrage," *Peace and Change* 33(1): 90–113.

Greenberg, K. J. (2009). *The Least Worst Place: Guantanamo's First 100 Days* (Oxford: Oxford University Press).

Greer, C., and E. McLaughlin (2010). "We Predict a Riot? Public Order Policing, New Media Environments and the Rise of the Citizen Journalist," *British Journal of Criminology* 50(6): 1041–1059.

Gregory, D. (2006). "The Black Flag: Guantánamo Bay and the Space of Exception," *Geografiska Annaler* 88(4): 405–427.

Grünfeld, F., and A. Huijboom (2007). *The Failure to Prevent Genocide in Rwanda: The Role of Bystanders* (Leiden: Martinus Nijhoff).

Grzyb, A. F. (2009). "Media Coverage, Activism, and Creating Public Will for Intervention in Rwanda and Darfur," in A. F. Grzyb (ed.), *The World and Darfur: International Response to Crimes against Humanity in Western Sudan* (Montreal: McGill-Queen's University Press), pp. 61–91.

Guantanamo Review Task Force (2010). "Final Report: Guantanamo Review Task Force," January 22, http://www.justice.gov/ag/guantanamo-review-final-report .pdf, accessed June 8, 2013.

Guidry, J. A., M. D. Kennedy, and M. N. Zald (eds.) (2000). *Globalizations and Social Movements: Culture, Power, and the Transnational Public Sphere* (Ann Arbor: University of Michigan Press).

Gunning, J. (2009). "Social Movement Theory and the Study of Terrorism," in R. Jackson, M. B. Smyth and J. Gunning (eds.), *Critical Terrorism Studies: Setting a New Research Agenda* (London: Routledge), pp. 156–177.

Gurney, C. (2000). "'A Great Cause': The Origins of the Anti-Apartheid Movement, June 1959–March 1960," *Journal of Southern African Studies* 26(1): 123–144.

Habermas, J. (1962/1989). *The Structural Transformation of the Public Sphere* (Cambridge, UK: Polity).

Haouas, I., E. Sayre, and M. Yagoubi (2012). "Youth Unemployment in Tunisia: Characteristics and Policy Responses," *Topics in Middle Eastern and African Economies* 14:395–415.

Hariman, R., and J. L. Lucaites (2007). *No Caption Needed: Iconic Photographs, Public Culture, and Liberal Democracy* (Chicago: University of Chicago Press).

Harris, Evan (2011). "Clinton Cites Rwanda, Bosnia in Rationale for Libya Intervention," *ABC News*, March 27, http://abcnews.go.com/blogs/politics /2011/03/clinton-cites-rwanda-bosnia-in-rationale-for-libya-intervention, accessed August 18, 2013.

Hart, S. (1996). "The Cultural Dimension of Social Movements: A Theoretical Assessment and Literature Review," *Sociology of Religion* 57(1): 87–100.

HBO (2010). "For Neda" (The New HBO Documentary Now Online), June 6, http://www.openculture.com/2010/06/for_neda_a_new_hbo_documentary. html, accessed May 29, 2013.

Held, D., A. McGrew, D. Goldblatt, and J. Perraton (1999). *Global Transformations: Politics, Economics, and Culture* (Cambridge, UK: Polity).

Hess, D., and B. Martin (2006). "Repression, Backfire, and the Theory of Transformative Events," *Mobilization* 11(2): 249–267.

Hobsbawn, E., and T. Ranger (eds.) (1983). *The Invention of Tradition* (Cambridge: Cambridge University Press).

Hornaday, A. (2005). "Room at the Inn: 'Hotel Rwanda' Heralds the Triumph of One Man's Decency," *Washington Post*, January 7, http://www.washingtonpost .com/wp-dyn/articles/A55029-2005Jan6.html, accessed May 5, 2010.

Houghton, D. P. (2001). *US Foreign Policy and the Iran Hostage Crisis* (Cambridge: Cambridge University Press).

*Huffington Post* (2013). "Navi Pillay, UN's Top Human Rights Official, Calls for Guantanamo Closing in Wake of Hunger Strikes," http://www.huffingtonpost. com/2013/04/05/navi-pillay-un-human-rights-guantanamo_n_3020494.html, accessed June 4, 2013.

Human Rights Watch (2004). "Darfur Destroyed," http://www.hrw.org/fr /node/12133/section/8, accessed June 1, 2011.

Human Rights Watch (2013a). "Facts and Figures: Military Commissions v. Federal Courts," http://www.hrw.org/features/guantanamo-facts-figures, accessed January 3, 2014.

Human Rights Watch (2013b). http://www.hrw.org/middle-eastn-africa/iran, accessed May 24, 2013.

Hyslop, J. (2014). "Mandela on War," in R. Barnard (ed.), *The Cambridge Companion to Nelson Mandela* (New York: Cambridge University Press), pp. 162–181.

International Campaign for Human Rights in Iran (2013). "Four Years Later, Still No Justice for Neda's Murder," http://www.iranhumanrights.org/2013/06 /neda_anniversary, accessed September 14, 2013.

International Defence and Aid Fund for Southern Africa (1978). *Nelson Mandela: The Struggle Is My Life* (London: International Defence and Aid Fund for Southern Africa).

Interview with the British Press (1990). http://www.sahistory.org.za/archive/inter view-british-press-johannesburg-march-1990, accessed April 12, 2013.

Iran Freedom Caravans (2009). http://iranfreedomcaravans.wordpress.com, accessed June 8, 2013.

Jasper, J. M. (1997). *The Art of Moral Protest* (Chicago: Chicago University Press).

Jasper, J. M. (2009). "Cultural Approaches in the Sociology of Social Movements," in B. Klandermans and C. Roggeband (eds.), *Handbook of Social Movements across Disciplines* (New York: Springer), pp. 59–109.

Jasper, J. M., and J. D. Poulsen (1995). "Recruiting Strangers and Friends: Moral Shocks and Social Networks in Animal Rights and Anti-Nuclear Protests," *Social Problems* 42(4): 493–512.

Johns, F. (2005). "Guantánamo Bay and the Annihilation of the Exception," *European Journal of International Law* 16(4): 613–635.

Johnston, H. (2009). "Protest Cultures: Performance, Artifacts, and Ideations," in H. Johnston (ed.), *Culture, Social Movements, and Protest* (Farnham: Ashgate), pp. 3–29.

Johnston, H., and B. Klandermans (eds.) (1995). *Social Movements and Culture* (Minneapolis: Regents of the University of Minnesota).

Juergensmeyer, M. (1987). "Saint Gandhi," in J. S. Hawley (ed.), *Saints and Virtues* (Berkeley: University of California Press), pp. 187–203.

Juergensmeyer, M. (2000). *Terror in the Mind of God* (Berkeley: University of California Press).

Juergensmeyer, M. (2005). "Religious Antiglobalism," in M. Juergensmeyer (ed.), *Religion in Global Civil Society* (Oxford: Oxford University Press), pp. 135–148.

Juris, J. S. (2008). *Networking Futures* (Durham, NC, and London: Duke University Press).

Kaldor, M. (2003). *Global Civil Society: An Answer to War* (Cambridge, UK: Polity).

Kane, J. (2001). *The Politics of Moral Capital* (Cambridge: Cambridge University Press).

Keck, M. E., and K. Sikkink (1998). *Activists beyond Borders: Advocacy Networks in International Politics* (Ithaca, NY, and London: Cornell University Press).

Kessler, G., and C. Lynch (2004). "U.S. Calls Killings in Sudan Genocide: Khartoum and Arab Militias Are Responsible, Powell Says," *Washington Post*, September 10, 2004.

Khan, I. (2005). "Report 2005: Foreword by Irene Khan, Secretary General," May 25, http://www.amnesty.org/en/library/asset/POL10/005/2005/en/82e61be8-d4f4-11dd-8a23-d58a49c0d652/pol100052005en.html, accessed June 5, 2013.

Khosrokhavar, F. (2005). *Suicide Bombers: Allah's New Martyrs* (London: Pluto).

Klapp, O. E. (1972). *Currents of Unrest: An Introduction to Collective Behavior* (New York: Holt, Rinehart, and Winston).

Klein, G. (2009). "The British Anti-Apartheid Movement and Political Prisoner Campaigns," *Journal of Southern African Studies* 35(2): 455–470.

Klotz, A. (1995). *Norms in International Relations: The Struggle against Apartheid* (Ithaca, NY: Cornell University Press).

Koopmans, R. (2004). "Movements and Media: Selection Processes and Evolutionary Dynamics in the Public Sphere," *Theory and Society* 33(3–4): 367–391.

Lahusen, C. (1996). *The Rhetoric of Moral Protest: Public Campaigns, Celebrity Endorsement, and Political Mobilization* (Berlin: Walter de Gruyter).

Lang, K., and G. E. Lang (1961). *Collective Dynamics* (New York: Thomas Y. Crowley).

Langenbacher, E., and Yossi Shain (eds.) (2010). *Power and the Past: Collective Memory and International Relations* (Washington, D C: Georgetown University Press).

Laustsen, C. B. (2006). "Med kameraet som våben: Om billederne fra Abu Ghraib," *Politica* 38(2): 187–209.

Levy, D., and N. Sznaider (2002). "Memory Unbound: The Holocaust and the Formation of Cosmopolitan Memory," *European Journal of Social Theory* 5(1): 87–106.

Liebes, T., and A. First (2003). "Framing the Palestinian-Israeli Conflict," in P. Norris, M. Kern, and M. Just (eds.), *Framing Terrorism: The News Media, the Government and the Public* (New York: Routledge), pp. 59–74.

Lim, M. (2013). "Framing Bouazizi: 'White Lies', Hybrid Network, and Collective/Connective Action in the 2010–11 Tunisian Uprising," *Journalism* 14(7): 921–941.

Lumsdaine, D. H. (1993). *Moral Vision in International Politics. The Foreign Aid Regime, 1949–1989* (Princeton, NJ: Princeton University Press).

Mackey, R. (2010). "Iranian TV Sees Conspiracy in Neda Video," *New York Times*, January 7, http://thelede.blogs.nytimes.com/2010/01/07/iranian-tv-sees -conspiracy-in-neda-video/?_r=0, accessed June 2, 2013.

Maclennan, B. (2010). "Lawyer Tells How He Tried to Cut Mandela Speech," *Mail and Guardian*, February 13, http://www.mg.co.za/article/2010-02-13-lawyer -tells-how-he-tried-to-cut-mandela-speech, accessed 12 June 2013.

Malcolm, A. (2009). "Iran Ambassador Suggests CIA Could Have Killed Neda Agha-Soltan," *Los Angeles Time*, June 25, http://latimesblogs.latimes.com /washington/2009/06/neda-cia-cnn-killing.html#more, accessed June 2, 2013.

Mandaville, P.G. (2003). *Transnational Muslim Politics: Reimagining the Umma* (New York: Routledge).

Mandela, N. (1964). "Nelson Mandela: 'I Am Prepared to Die'" (Nelson Mandela's Statement from the Dock at the Opening of the Defence Case in the Rivonia Trial), http://www.historyplace.com/speeches/mandela.htm, accessed August 1, 2013.

Mandela, N. (1990a). "Mandela's Wembley speech," http://www.sahistory.org.za /topic/nelson-mandelas-wembley-speech, accessed August 4, 2013.

Mandela, N. (1990b). "Address of the Deputy President of the African National Congress Nelson Mandela, at the European parliament Strasbourg, 13 June 1990," http://www.sahistory.org.za/archive/address-deputy-president-african -national-congress-nelson-mandela-european-parliament-strasb, accessed March 12, 2013.

Margalit, A. (2002). *The Ethics of Memory* (Cambridge, MA: Harvard University Press).

Martin, B. (2005). "The Beating of Rodney King: The Dynamics of Backfire," *Critical Criminology,* 13(3): 307–326.

McAdam, D. (1982/1999). *Political Process and the Development of Black Insurgency, 1930–1970* (Chicago: Chicago University Press).

McAdam, D. (2000). "Movement Strategy and Dramaturgic Framing in Democratic States: The Case of the American Civil Rights Movement," in S. Chambers and A. Costain (eds.), *Deliberation, Democracy and the Media* (Lanham, MD: Rowman and Littlefield), pp. 117–133.

McAdam, D., and D. Rucht (1993). "The Cross-National Diffusion of Movement Ideas," *Annals of the American Academy of Political and Social Science* 528:56–74.

McCain, J. (2009). "John McCain Tribute to Neda on the Senate Floor," June 22, http://www.youtube.com/watch?v=lp5ApDTfsTM, accessed May 31, 2013.

McDonald, K. (2006). *Global Movements: Action and Culture* (Malden, MA: Blackwell).

Melvern, L. (2000). *A People Betrayed: The Role of the West in Rwanda's Genocide* (London: Zed Books).

Menchú, R., with E. Burgos-Debray (1984). *Rigoberta Menchú: An Indian Woman in Guatemala* (London: Verso).

Moore, Jr. B. (1978). *Injustice: The Social Bases of Obedience and Revolt* (London and Basingstoke: Macmillan).

Mortensen, M. (2011). "When Citizen Photojournalism Sets the News Agenda: Neda Agha Soltan as a Web 2.0 Icon of Post-Election Unrest in Iran," *Global Media and Communication* 7(1): 4–16.

Mozaffari, M. (2007). 'What Is Islamism?: History and Definition of a Concept," *Totalitarian Movements and Political Religions* 8(1): 17–33.

Müller, J-W. (ed.) (2002). *Memory and Power in Post-War Europe* (Cambridge: Cambridge University Press).

Mutasa, C. (2004). "Global Apartheid," *Global Policy Forum*, September 9, http://www.globalpolicy.org/component/content/article/210/44769.html, accessed May 2, 2011.

Naghibi, N. (2011). "Diasporic Disclosures: Social Networking, Neda, and the 2009 Iranian Presidential Elections," *Biography* 34(1): 56–69.

*New York Times* (1990). "South Africa's New Era; Transcript of Mandela's Speech at Cape Town City Hall: 'Africa It Is Ours!,'" February 12, http://www.nytimes.com/1990/02/12/world/south-africa-s-new-era-transcript-mandela-s-speech-cape-town-city-hall-africa-it.html?pagewanted=all&src=pm, accessed August 20, 2013.

*New York Times* (2004). "Time for Action on Sudan," June 18, http://www.nytimes.com/2004/06/18/opinion/time-for-action-on-sudan.html, accessed March 3, 2010.

Nixon, R. (1991). "Mandela, Messianism, and the Media," *Transition* 51:42–55.

Nora, P. (ed.) (1996). *Realms of Memory*, Vol. 1 (New York: Columbia University Press).

Obama, B. (2010). "News Conference by the President," December 22, http://www.whitehouse.gov/the-press-office/2010/12/22/news-conference-president, accessed June 4, 2013.

Olesen, T. (2005). *International Zapatismo: The Construction of Solidarity in the Age of Globalization* (London: Zed Books).

Olesen, T. (2007a). "Contentious Cartoons: Elite and Media Driven Mobilization," *Mobilization* 12(1): 37–52.

Olesen, T. (2007b). "The Porous Public and the Transnational Dialectic," *Acta Sociologica* 50(3): 295–308.

Olesen, T. (2009). "The Muhammad Cartoons Conflict and Transnational Activism," *Ethnicities* 9(3): 409–426.

Olesen, T. (2011). "Transnational Injustice Symbols and Communities: The Case of al-Qaeda and the Guantanamo Bay Detention Camp," *Current Sociology* 59(6): 717–734.

Olesen, T. (2013a). "Injustice Symbols: On the Political-Cultural Outcomes of Social Movements," Paper Presented at the ECPR General Conference, Bordeaux, September 4–7, 2013.

Olesen, T. (2013b). "'We Are All Khaled Said': On Visual Injustice Symbols," *Research in Social Movements, Conflicts, and Change* 35:3–25.

Olesen, T. (2013c). "Dramatic Diffusion and Injustice Symbols: The Case of Mohamed Bouazizi and the Tunisian Revolution, 2010–2011," Paper Presented at the ECPR Joint Sessions Workshop, Mainz, March 11–16, 2013.

Olesen, T. (2014). "From National Event to Transnational Injustice Symbol: The Three Phases of the Muhammad Cartoons Controversy," in L. Bosi, C. Demetriou, and S. Malthaner (eds.), *Dynamics of Political Violence* (Farnham: Ashgate).

Olick, J. K. (2007). *The Politics of Regret: On Collective Memory and Historical Responsibility* (New York: Routledge).

Olick, J. K., V. Vinitzky-Seroussi, and D. Levy (2011). "Introduction," in J. K. Olick, V. Vinitzky-Seroussi, and D. Levy (eds.), *The Collective Memory Reader* (Oxford: Oxford University Press), pp. 3–62.

Perryman, M. (1988). "The Mandela Moment," *Marxism Today*, September 28–31.

PET [the Danish Security and Intelligence Service] (2009). "Tegningesagen i al-Qaida's ideologiske perspektiv" [The Muhammad Cartoons Case in the Ideological Perspective of al-Quaida], https://www.pet.dk/CTA/-/media/Publikationer/AQ_tegninger.ashx, accessed August 14, 2013.

Pipes, D. (2003). *The Rushdie Affair: The Novel, the Ayatollah, and the West*, 2nd ed. (New Brunswick, NJ: Transaction).

Pleyers, G. (2010). *Alter-Globalization: Becoming Actors in a Global Age* (Oxford: Polity).

Poole, R. (2008). "Memory, History, and the Claims of the Past," *Memory Studies* 1(2): 149–166.

Putz, U. (2009). "Neda, Is She Iran's Joan of Arc?," *ABC News*, June 22, http://abc news.go.com/International/story?id=7897043&page=1, accessed June 1, 2013.

Reitan, Ruth (2007). *Global Activism* (London: Routledge).

Reuters (2013). "Zawahri Vows al Qaeda to Free Guantanamo Inmates," July 31, http://www.reuters.com/article/2013/07/31/us-usa-qaeda-guantanamo-idUS BRE96U07K20130731, accessed October 9, 2013.

Robertson, R. (1992). *Globalization: Social Theory and Global Culture* (London: Sage).

Rogan, H. (2007). "Abu Reuter and the E-Jihad: Virtual Battlefronts from Iraq to the Horn of Africa," *Georgetown Journal of International Affairs* (Summer/Fall): 89–96.

Roy, O. (2004). *Globalised Islam: The Search for a New Ummah* (London: Hurst).

Rucht, D. (1999). "The Transnationalization of Social Movements: Trends, Causes, and Problems," in D. della Porta, H. Kriesi, and D. Rucht (eds.), *Social Movements in a Globalizing World* (Houndmills and London: Macmillan), pp. 206–222.

Rucht, D. (2004). "The Quadruple 'A': Media Strategies of Protest Movements since the 1960s," in W. van de Bonk, B. D. Loader, P. G. Nixon, and D. Rucht (eds.), *Cyber Protest: New Media, Citizens, and Social Movements* (London: Routledge), pp. 29–56.

Russell, A. (2011). *Networked: A Contemporary History of News in Transition* (Cambridge, UK: Polity).

Ryan, Y. (2011). "The Tragic Life of a Street Vendor," *Al-Jazeera*, January 20, www.aljazeera.com/indepth/features/2011/01/201111684242518839.html, accessed December 11, 2012.

Sageman, M. (2004). *Understanding Terror Networks* (Philadelphia: University of Pennsylvania Press).

Sageman, M. (2008). *Leaderless Jihad: Terror Networks in the Twenty-first Century* (Philadelphia: University of Pennsylvania Press).

Said, Edward (1978). *Orientalism* (New York: Random House).

Sampson, A. (1999). *Mandela: The Authorised Biography* (London: Harper Collins).

Sanders, J. (2000). *South Africa and the International Media, 1972–1979: A Struggle for Representation* (London: Frank Cass).

Schlegel, A. (1995). "My Lai: 'We Lie, They Die' or, a Small History of an 'Atrocious' Photograph," *Third Text* 9(31): 47–66.

Schmid, A. P., and J. de Graaf (1982). *Violence as Communication: Insurgent Terrorism and the Western News Media* (London: Sage).

Schraeder, P. J., and H. Redissi (2011). "Ben Ali's Fall," *Journal of Democracy* 22(3): 5–19.

Schwartz, B. (1990). "The Reconstruction of Abraham Lincoln," in D. Middleton and D. Edwards (eds.), *Collective Remembering* (London: Sage), pp. 81–107.

Sejerstad, F. (1993). "Award Ceremony Speech," http://www.nobelprize.org/nobel_prizes/peace/laureates/1993/presentation-speech.html, accessed June 8, 2012.

Sengupta, K. (2011). "How Revolution Turned Sour in the Birthplace of the Arab Spring," *Independent*, September 28, www.independent.co.uk/news/world/africa/how-revolution-turned-sour-in-the-birthplace-of-the-arab-spring-2362060.html, accessed January 16, 2013.

Shavit, U. (2009). *The New Imagined Community: Global Media and the Construction of National and Muslim Identities of Migrants* (Brighton: Sussex Academic).

Shaw, M. (2000). *Theory of the Global State* (Cambridge: Cambridge University Press).

Sikkink, K., and J. Smith (2002). "Infrastructures for Change: Transnational Organizations, 1953–93," in S. Khagram, J. V. Riker, and K. Sikkink (eds.), *Restructuring World Politics: Transnational Social Movements, Networks, and Norms* (Minneapolis: University of Minnesota Press), pp. 24–44.

Silverstone, R. (2007). *Media and Morality: On the Rise of the Mediapolis* (Cambridge, UK: Polity).

Skinner, R. (2009). "The Moral Foundations of British Anti-Apartheid Activism, 1946–1960," *Journal of Southern African Studies* 35(2): 399–416.

Smith, A. D. (1990). "Towards a Global Culture," *Theory, Culture and Society* 7:171–191.

Smith, A. D. (1995). *Nations and Nationalism in a Global Era* (Cambridge, MA: Blackwell).

Smith, J. (2008) *Social Movements for Global Democracy* (Baltimore, MD: Johns Hopkins University Press).

Smith, J., C. Chatfield, and R. Pagnucco (eds.) (1997). *Transnational Social Movements and Global Politics: Solidarity beyond the State* (Syracuse, NY: Syracuse University Press).

Smith, J., and H. Johnston (eds.) (2002). *Globalization and Resistance: Transnational Dimensions of Social Movements* (Lanham, MD: Rowman and Littlefield).

Smith, Philip (2000). "Culture and Charisma: Outline of a Theory," *Acta Sociologica* 43(2): 101–111.

Smith, P., and J. C. Alexander (2005). "Introduction: The New Durkheim," in J. C. Alexander and P. Smith (eds.), *The Cambridge Companion to Durkheim* (Cambridge: Cambridge University Press), pp. 1–37.

Snow, D. A., E. B. Rochford, Jr., S. K. Worden, and R. D. Benford (1986). "Frame Alignment Processes, Micromobilization, and Movement Participation," *American Sociological Review* 51(4): 464–481.

Snow, D. A., and R. D. Benford (1988). "Ideology, Frame Resonance, and Participant Mobilization," in B. Klandermans, H. Kriesi, and S. Tarrow (eds.), *From Structure to Action: Comparing Social Movement Research across Cultures*, International Social Movement Research 1 (Greenwich: JAI), pp. 197–217.

Snow, D. A., and R. D. Benford (1992). "Master Frames and Cycles of Protest," in A. D. Morris and C. McCluerg Mueller (eds.), *Frontiers in Social Movement Theory* (New Haven, CT: Yale University Press), pp. 133–155.

Snow, D. A., and R. D. Benford (1999). "Alternative Types of Cross-National Diffusion in the Social Movement Arena," in D. della Porta, H. Kriesi, and D. Rucht (eds.), *Social Movements in a Globalizing World* (Houndmills: Macmillan), pp. 23–39.

Snow, D. A., and S. C. Byrd (2007). "Ideology, Framing Processes, and Islamic Terrorist Movements," *Mobilization* 12(2): 119–136.

Snow, D. A., and S. A. Soule (2010). *A Primer on Social Movements* (New York: W. W. Norton).

Sontag, S. (2003). *At betragte andres lidelser* (København: Tiderne Skifter).

Spivak, G. (1988). "Can the Subaltern Speak?," in C. Nelson and L. Grossberg (eds.), *Marxism and the Interpretation of Culture* (Chicago: University of Illinois Press), pp. 271–313.

Stage, C. (2011). "Thingifying Neda: The Construction of Commemorative and Affective Thingfications of Neda Agda Soltan," *Culture Unbound* 3:419–438.

Stoll, D. (1999). *Rigoberta Menchú and the Story of All Poor Guatemalans* (Boulder, CO: Westview).

Strömbäck, J. (2005). "In Search of a Standard: Four Models of Democracy and Their Normative Implications for Journalism," *Journalism Studies* 6(3): 331–345.

Stultz, N. M. (1991). "Evolution of the United Nations Anti-Apartheid Regime," *Human Rights Quarterly* 13(1): 1–23.

Swidler, A. (1986). "Culture in Action: Symbols and Strategies," *American Sociological Review* 52(2): 273–286.

Sznaider, N. (2001). *The Compassionate Temperament: Care and Cruelty in Modern Society* (Lanham, MD: Rowman and Littlefield).

Tait, R. (2012). "Iran Resurrects Salman Rushdie Threat," *Telegraph*, September 16, http://www.telegraph.co.uk/news/worldnews/middleeast/iran/9546513/Iran-resurrects-Salman-Rushdie-threat.html, accessed June 12, 2013.

Tait, R., and M. Weaver (2009). "The Accidental Martyr," *Guardian*, June 23.

Tambo, O. (1965/1973). "Introduction," in R. First (ed.), *Nelson Mandela, No Easy Walk to Freedom* (London: Heinemann), pp. ix–xiv.

Tarrow, S. (1998). *Power in Movement: Social Movements and Contentious Politics*, 2nd ed. (Cambridge: Cambridge University Press).

Tarrow, S. (2005). *The New Transnational Activism* (Cambridge: Cambridge University Press).

Taylor, J. (1998). *Body Horror: Photojournalism, Catastrophe and War* (Manchester: Manchester University Press).

Teune, S. (ed.) (2010). *The Transnational Condition: Protest Dynamics in an Entangled Europe* (New York: Berghahn).

Thompson, A. (ed.) (2007). *The Media and the Rwanda Genocide* (London: Pluto).

Thompson, J. B. (1995). *The Media and Modernity: A Social Theory of the Media* (Cambridge, UK: Polity).

Thörn, H. (2006). *Anti-Apartheid and the Emergence of a Global Civil Society* (Basingstoke: Palgrave Macmillan).

Thörn, H. (2009). "The Meaning(s) of Solidarity: Narratives of Anti-Apartheid Activism," *Journal of Southern African Studies* 35(2): 417–436.

Tilly, C. (1978). *From Mobilization to Revolution* (New York: McGraw-Hill).

Tomaselli, K., and B. Boster (1993). "Mandela, MTV, Television and Apartheid," *Popular Music and Society* 17(2): 1–19.

Torpey, J. (ed.) (2003). *Politics and the Past: On Repairing Historical Injustice* (Lanham, MD: Rowman and Littlefield).

Totten, M. J. (2012). "The Woman Who Blew up the Arab World," May 17, www.worldaffairsjournal.org/blog/michael-j-totten/woman-who-blew-arab-world, accessed December 19, 2012.

Tuman, J. S. (2010). *Communicating Terror: The Rhetorical Dimensions of Terrorism*, 2nd ed. (Thousand Oaks, CA: Sage).

Turner, R. H., and L. M. Killian (1957). *Collective Behavior* (Englewood Cliffs, NJ: Prentice-Hall).

Turner, V. (1967). *Forest of Symbols; Aspects of Ndembu ritual* (Ithaca, NY: Cornell University Press).

UN (1994). "United Nations Security Council Resolution 955 Establishing the International Tribunal for Rwanda (with Annexed Statute)" (Adopted by the Security Council at Its 3453rd Meeting), November 8, http://www1.umn.edu/humanrts/peace/docs/scres955.html, accessed June 5, 2011.

UN (2003). "International Day of Reflection on the 1994 Genocide in Rwanda" (Resolution 58/234, Adopted by the General Assembly), December 23, http://www.preventgenocide.org/prevent/UNdocs/UNGAResOn10th AnniversaryOfGenocideInRwanda.htm, accessed June 5, 2011.

UN (2010). "Security Council Establishes Residual Mechanism to Conclude Tasks of International Criminal Tribunals for Rwanda, Former Yugoslavia," December 22, http://www.un.org/News/Press/docs/2010/sc10141.doc.htm, accessed June 3, 2011.

Vandeginste, S. (2003). "Victims of Genocide, Crimes against Humanity, and War Crimes in Rwanda: The Legal and Institutional Framework of Their Right to Reparation," in J. Torpey (ed.), *Politics and the Past: On Repairing Historical Injustice* (Lanham, MD: Rowman and Littlefield), pp. 249–274.

Waters, M. (1995). *Globalization* (London: Routledge).

Wennerhag, M. (2008). *Global rörelse: Den globala rättviserörelsen och modernitetens omvandlinger* (Stockholm: Atlas).

Whitney, C. R. (1998). "At Inquiry, French Officials Say They Tried in Rwanda," *New York Times*, April 22.

Wickham, C. R. (2005). "The Islamist Alternative to Globalization," in M. Juergensmeyer (ed.), *Religion in Global Civil Society* (Oxford: Oxford University Press), pp. 149–169.

Williams, R. H. (2004). "The Cultural Context of Collective Action: Constraints, Opportunities, and the Symbolic Life of Social Movements," in D. A. Snow, S. A. Soule, and H. Kriesi (eds.), *The Blackwell Companion to Social Movements* (Oxford, UK: Blackwell), pp. 91–115.

Worthington, A. (2007). *The Guantánamo Files: The Stories of the 759 Detainees in America's Illegal Prison* (London: Pluto).

Wrong, M. (2005). "Horror Movies," *Guardian*, February 18, 2005.

Zehfuss, M. (2007). *Wounds of Memory: The Politics of War in Germany* (Cambridge: Cambridge University Press).

Zelizer, B. (2010). *About to Die: How News Images Move the Public* (New York: Oxford University Press).

Zuo, J., and R. D. Benford (1995). "Mobilization Processes and the 1989 Chinese Democracy Movement," *The Sociological Quarterly* 36(1): 131–156.

# INDEX

Lightning Source UK Ltd.
Milton Keynes UK
UKOW06n1823100415

249444UK00004B/83/P